Beyond the Culture Wars

Books by Gerald Graff

Poetic Statement and Critical Dogma

Literature against Itself: Literary Ideas in Modern Society

Professing Literature: An Institutional History

Beyond the Culture Wars

*How
Teaching the Conflicts
Can Revitalize
American Education*
Gerald Graff

W · W · Norton & Company

New York   London

First Edition

The text of this book is composed in 11/13.5 Berkeley Old Style Book
with the display set in Berkeley Old Style Medium.
Composition and manufacturing by The Maple-Vail Book Manufacturing Group.
Book design by Margaret M. Wagner.

Library of Congress Cataloging-in-Publication Data
Graff, Gerald.
beyond the culture wars : how teaching the conflicts
can revitalize american education / Gerald Graff. — 1st ed.
p.   cm.
Includes bibliographical references and index.
1. Education, Higher—Social aspects—United States.
2. Universities and colleges—United States—Curricula.   I. Title.
LC191.4.G73   1992
370.19—dc20   92–12855

ISBN 0–393–03424–0

W. W. Norton & Company, Inc.
500 Fifth Avenue, New York, N.Y. 10110
W. W. Norton & Company Ltd.
10 Coptic Street, London WC1A 1PU

1   2 3 4 5 6 7 8 9 0

Contents

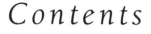

Preface

WRITING for a general audience is not an easy thing for the average academic. As writers we academics are spoiled. We are used to writing for other academics, usually those in our particular fields, and this protection from outside perspectives lets us fall into cozy ways of thinking and expressing ourselves. You might think that our students would provide the outside perspective that would force us to make ourselves clearer to nonacademics, but students after all are captive audiences and are not always in a position to tell us when we aren't making sense.

You would also think that the increasingly contentious atmosphere of the campus these days would smoke us out of our academic foxholes and make us come to the point. To an extent this is just what is happening today, as the recent deluge of vituperative attacks on changes in the academy are forcing those on the receiving end to try to get their side of the story into the news. Nevertheless, whenever clarity threatens to break out about our academic practices, the very organization of academic life works against it. The insularity of my department, my courses, and my circle of professional contacts tends to protect me from the need to talk to anyone who doesn't already see things pretty much the way I do or who disagrees with me only from within assumptions that others would not share. Such an environment is pleasant, but it strikes me as poor training for dealing with a world in which a lot of people don't see things the way I do and might even find my way of seeing them pretty bizarre.

So the problems I have had in writing this book turn out to be intimately connected with the problems the book is about— namely, the communicative disorders of a society that is becoming so shell-shocked by cultural conflict and disagreement that it would rather escape from the battle than confront it and try to work things out. For finally, the habit of preaching to the already converted is not restricted to the academy. A dangerous inability to talk to one another is the price we pay for a culture that makes it easy for us to avoid having to respect and deal with the people who strongly disagree with us. Like the American university, a good deal of American life is organized so as to protect us from having to confront those unpleasant adversaries who may be just the ones we need to listen to.

All this is a roundabout way of saying that I drew on a lot of help in writing this book, people who helped me write my way out of my cozy academic habits without, I hope, losing whatever is valuable in the academic perspective, and that the crucial help came from people who represented an "outside" view of one kind or another. These included academics on the leftist side of the debate that has so polarized us in the culture war, academics whom I attacked for many years—in books like *Literature against Itself: Literary Ideas in Modern Society,* which was published in 1979 and made me for a while the hero of the war against academic "theory"—until it dawned on me that I was learning more from my adversaries than from my allies. The seemingly counter-intuitive arguments I had been attacking, I came to recognize, are often overstatements of neglected insights. As this book will try to show, to dismiss these arguments with sneers and ridicule is simply to close ourselves off from new ways of thinking.

Gregory Jay of the University of Wisconsin at Milwaukee has been central among those who were formerly opponents. Greg's comments on endless drafts of my manuscript were often so incisive that I finally decided at several points simply to quote them in the text, attributing them to a book in progress on the culture of democracy that he tells me he now actually intends to write. Jeff Rice of Great Expectations bookstore in Evanston, Illinois, also went beyond the call of duty by reading numerous drafts and showing me how to rewrite them. So did Bonnie Auslander, who extended her duties as director of the Writing Center at Converse College of Spartanburg, South Carolina, to give me a writing lesson. Others who contributed to my thinking and writing include Dana Polan, William E. Cain, Bill Haddad, John Schilb, Gavin Witt, and Charles Newman.

For a different kind of "outside" perspective, I am in debt to my editor at W. W. Norton, Henning Gutmann, who was instrumental in the conception, shaping, and execution of this project at all points. Henning's infinite patience with an obsessive reviser of manuscripts (and a FAX machine with which to inflict them on editors) is something I will always be grateful for, as well as for his steadiness in putting me back on track when I wandered into unpromising byways.

A book that is so much about the "outside" perspective of students could obviously not have been written without a lot of help from them, particularly my undergraduate and graduate students at Northwestern University and the University of Chicago, who have obligingly let me test my educational ideas on them in my classes and given me their frank reactions. Educational literature has long been haunted by an elusive fictional character called "the student" (or "the struggling student," as this character is often called in my pages), who at times actually bears a remote resemblance to the real human beings who show up in our courses. I hope my own students will be able to recognize some of their own and their classmates' actual experience in my broad sketch.

I would also like to thank the numerous colleges and universities that invited me to speak and in some cases advise them on the reform of their curricula. In the latter category I want particularly to thank the faculty and administrators who entertained me at the University of North Carolina at Greensboro (with special gratitude to Associate Dean Henry Levinson), Dickinson College, Valparaiso University, Carnegie Mellon University, and the University of Colorado.

Finally, in a book so directly about the positive potential of controversy for the vitality of culture and education, I would be remiss if I did not thank the conservatives with whom I persistently take issue throughout this book. In particular I wish to thank the National Association of Scholars for the invitation to speak at its national conference, an occasion that produced the talk on teaching Joseph Conrad's *Heart of Darkness* that is now part of Chapter 2. Nobody ever gets to choose his adversaries, and we should feel honored by those who attack us even if we think the attack is unfair. With luck, we academics who have been coming under fire in the culture war will someday be able to look back at our critics and say, "Thanks, we needed that."

Gerald Graff
Chicago, Illinois
March 1992

Beyond the Culture Wars

Chapter 1

Introduction:
Conflict in America

I F WE believe what we have been reading lately, American higher education is in a disastrous state. As pictured in a stream of best sellers, commission reports, polemical articles, and editorials, the academic humanities in particular look like a once-respectable old neighborhood gone bad. The stately old buildings have been defaced with spray paint, hideous accumulations of trash litter the ground, and omnipresent thought police control the turf, speaking in barbarous, unintelligible tongues while enforcing an intolerant code of political correctness on the terrorized inhabitants.

Having lived in this neighborhood for the last thirty years as a teacher of literature, a department chair, a lecturer at numerous universities, and a curriculum consultant at some, I find it hard to square these lurid accounts with my experience. As my first chapter illustrates, there is something truly astonishing about the degree of exaggeration, patent falsehood, and plain hysteria attained by the more prominent of these accounts. Much of the hysteria comes from simple fear of change, but much of it comes from the mysterious nature of certain precincts of the academic world to both other academics and the public. When a country is little known, fabulous and monstrous tales readily circulate about it, and any abuse can be passed off as typical.

It is true that staggering changes have occurred in the climate of academic life over the course of my professional life. I started graduate school in 1959, so my career spans the abyss between today's feverish struggles over books and the days when the literary canon—the body of literature thought to be worth teaching—seemed so uncontroversial that you rarely heard the word "canon." It is also true that social and cultural change has brought difficult new problems in the areas of admissions, hiring, and campus life. In my view, however, these are the problems of success, a consequence of the vast superiority of today's university in intellectual reach and cultural diversity to the relatively restricted campus culture of a generation ago. That today's university is rocked by unprecedented conflicts is a measure of its vitality, not its decline. As I see it, the challenge is to turn these very conflicts to positive account, by transforming a scene of hatred and anger into one of educationally productive debate. How this can be done is the subject of this book.

Though I am sympathetic to feminism, multiculturalism, and other new theories and practices that have divided the academy, I do not argue that these movements have the final word about culture—only that the questions they are raising deserve to be taken seriously. Yet one would never guess from the overheated and ill-informed accounts given by today's popular critics that the issues in the battle over education are ones on which reasonable people might legitimately disagree. Arguments that at the very least are worthy of debate—like the argument that political factors such as race, class, gender, and nationality have influenced art and criticism far more than education has traditionally acknowledged—have been reduced by their opponents to their crudest and most strident form and thus dismissed without a hearing (see Chapters 2 and 8). A complex set of issues that cry out for serious debate has been turned into a clear-cut choice—

as one prominent conservative puts it—"between culture and barbarism."[1]

No doubt it pleases such critics to think of themselves as last-ditch defenders of civilization against the invasion of barbarian relativists and terrorists. But if the goal is constructive educational reform, then such apocalyptic posturing is a dead end. One does not have to be a tenured radical to see that what has taken over the educational world today is not barbarism and unreason but, simply, conflict. The first step in dealing productively with today's conflicts is to recognize their legitimacy.

This book asks us to rethink the premise that the eruption of fundamental conflict in education has to mean educational and cultural paralysis. My argument is that conflict has to mean paralysis only as long as we fail to take positive advantage of it.

Acknowledging the legitimacy of social conflict, however, is not an easy thing even for Americans of goodwill. We may not hesitate to embrace cultural diversity, but when diversity leads to clashes of interests, as it naturally will, we find ourselves at a loss. Such conflict seems vaguely un-American, a legacy of the less abundant societies of the Old World. President Bush echoed an old American tradition when he recently declared that class conflict is "for European democracies . . . it isn't for the United States of America. We are not going to be divided by class."[2]

In fact, there is little reason to think we Americans are any less divided by class than other nations, but we are certainly better at concealing it from ourselves. A combination of affluence and geography has enabled more fortunate Americans to avoid noticing unpleasant social conflicts by the simple device of moving away from them. In times past there was the frontier, settled mostly by conquerable Indian tribes, to which Americans could flee when urban conflict became too intense. More recently the flight has been out to suburbs and malls, on freeways which let us drive past our social problems, or into high rises from which those problems need be viewed only from a distance.

In our mass-produced fantasies we are virtually obsessed with conflict, but of a stylized, unreal, or commercially trivialized kind. Our popular films and television programs often deal with the sorts of conflicts that can be resolved by a fistfight, a car chase, or a shoot-out at the OK Corral. Our TV commercials stage endless disputations between partisans of old and new improved brands of soap, toothpaste, or deodorant, including the great debate over whether we should drink a particular beer because it is Less Filling or because it Tastes Great. Other commercials present modern life as a conflict-free utopia in which races freely intermingle and the world's ethnic groups join hands on a hillside to hymn their desire to buy the world a Coke. Our national obsession with athletic contests (one I fully share) is at least partly explained by the fact that conflict in sports, unlike in real life, is safe and satisfying, with clear-cut winners and losers.

Lately, however, conflicts over race, gender, and ethnicity have become so frequent and conspicuous that we seem to be getting more accustomed to dealing with them. This is seen in the public fascination with social-conflict films like *Do the Right Thing, Thelma and Louise,* and *Dances with Wolves* and with events like the Clarence Thomas-Anita Hill sexual harassment hearings. Yet the same conflicts that we have begun to accept in society still stick in our craw when they appear in education. The race, class, and gender conflicts that national newsmagazines treat as understandable and legitimate in films and public hearings have been depicted by these same magazines as a catastrophe for education.

Clearly, we still long to think of education as a conflict-free ivory tower, and the university *tries* to live up to this vision. While it welcomes diversity and innovation, it neutralizes the conflicts which result from them. This it does by keeping warring parties in noncommunicating courses and departments and by basing the curriculum on a principle of live and let live: I won't try to prevent you from teaching and studying what you want if you don't try to prevent me from teaching and studying what I want.

The effects of this amiable rule of laissez-faire have by no means been all bad, and it would be a serious mistake to try to abolish it entirely. It has enabled the American curriculum to relieve the increasingly conflicting pressures placed on it by painlessly expanding its frontiers, adding new subjects, courses, and programs without asking those in control of the already established ones to change their ways. It is only by such peaceful coexistence that the university could have achieved the improbable feat of becoming modern society's chief patron of cultural innovation without ceasing to stand for staunchly traditional values.[3]

As I point out in Chapter 7, the modern university has from the beginning rested on a deeply contradictory mission. The university is expected to preserve, transmit, and honor our traditions, yet at the same time it is supposed to produce new knowledge, which means questioning received ideas and perpetually revising traditional ways of thinking. The smooth functioning of the modern university has depended on a silent agreement to minimize this conflict between old and new, and times of relative affluence have afforded the room to pursue both missions without fatal collisions. This explains how it is possible for both the left and the right to believe with some reason that the opposing party is in charge.

Today, however, we see the end of the growth economy that for so long enabled the university to cushion its conflicts by indefinitely expanding the departmental and curricular playing field. Meanwhile, the contradictions that have accumulated as the academy has diversified have become so deep, antagonistic, and openly political that it has become impossible to prevent them from becoming visible to outsiders. In no other American institution do we find such a mind-boggling juxtaposition of clashing ideologies: corporate managers side by side with third world Marxists; free market economists with free-form sculptors; mandarin classical scholars with postmodern performance artists; football coaches with deconstructive feminists. Peaceful coexistence is increasingly strained, and it is harder to hold the conflicts at bay by the silent agreement not to wash dirty linen in public.

The result is today's educational crisis. It is a sign of the university's vitality that the crisis is happening so openly there. The academic curriculum has become a prominent arena of cultural conflict because it is a microcosm, as it should be, of the clash of cultures and values in America as a whole. As the democratization of culture has brought heretofore excluded groups into the educational citadel, with them have come the social conflicts that their exclusion once kept safely distant. A generation ago decisions about what was worth teaching and what counted as "culture" were still circumscribed by a relatively homogeneous class with a relatively common background. Today new constituencies—women, blacks, gays, and immigrant groups from Asia and Latin America in particular—demand a say in how culture will be defined. And even more offensive to those who are used to having their way without controversy, these upstarts are now often in a position to put their ideas into practice. A less "canonical" faculty and student body implies a less canonical curriculum, dramatizing the fact that culture itself is a debate, not a monologue.[4]

Never comfortable with conflict to begin with, we are naturally prone to interpret these challenges as symptoms of disintegration. Many of the well-publicized horror stories about intolerant political correctness on campus—when they have not been shown to be simply bogus[5]—seem to me a symptom not of left-wing McCarthyism, as has been charged, but of fear in the face of controversy. In some cases, at least, I believe that what teachers have perceived as "harassment" is simply the novel experience of being in a minority and having to argue for one's beliefs instead of taking them for granted. Some overzealous proponents of cultural diversity have indeed behaved obnox-iously in attempting to sensitize their student and faculty col-leagues whether they wish to be sensitized or not. But it is not necessarily a symptom of intolerance if a feminist student chal-lenges a teacher's interpretation of Henry James for acceding to a stereotype about women or if a black student asks why a slave diary has not been assigned in a course on the Civil War.

I suspect that the teachers who have reacted to such criticisms by canceling their courses and offering themselves to the media as helpless victims of political correctness would have done bet-ter to stay and argue the issues with their students. Good teach-ers, after all, *want* their students to talk back. They know that student docility is a far more pervasive problem than student intransigence. Good students for their part appreciate teachers who take strong positions on controversial questions—though they do not appreciate brainwashing.

If the public furor over political correctness has shed more heat than light, it has at least proved that the gap between Amer-ican culture and the ivory tower has closed. There is an old joke that academic disputes are especially poisonous because so little is at stake in them. But the stakes are no longer so trivial: Today's academic disputes over which texts should be taught in the humanities, over the competing claims of Western and non-Western culture, and over the pros and cons of affirmative action and codes regulating hate speech mirror broader social conflicts over race, ethnicity, and privilege. Even the quarrels sparked by esoteric literary theories about the pertinence of gender ques-tions to the study of Shakespeare echo debates over sex roles in the larger society provoked by feminists, gay activists, and the entry of women into the professional work force. At a moment when many in our society are questioning traditional assump-tions about romantic love, heterosexuality, the nuclear family, abortion, aging, free speech, and the American flag, we should not be too outraged that decisions about which books to assign no longer go without saying.

But if outrage is not a helpful response to the conflicts occasioned by new interests, ideas, and constituencies, neither is the liberal complacency that has been content to say, "Sure, we can handle that innovation; we'll just add a new course on it." The current educational crisis has exposed the limitations of the live-and-let-live philosophy of curriculum, enabling conservatives to take the lead in the education debate and attract many disillusioned liberals to their side. The conservatives speak powerfully because they recognize the incoherence of a curriculum that is content to go on endlessly multiplying courses and subjects like boutiques at a mall. Unfortunately the conservatives' only prescription for curing this incoherence is to superimpose a higher order on the curriculum, an order that they like to call the "common culture" but that is really only *their* idea of order, one contender among several competing ones.

The history of modern American education has pitted the liberal pluralist solution (everyone do his or her own thing) against the conservative solution (everyone do the conservatives' thing). What is happening, today, I believe, is that both the liberal pluralist and the conservative solutions have outlived their usefulness. Everyone doing his or her own thing has made a mess of the curriculum, but cleaning up the mess by reverting to a narrowly defined traditional curriculum can only make a far worse mess. Since such a traditional curriculum would mean cutting away the vast areas of the world of knowledge and culture that do not fit the conservative vision of reality, it could be institutionalized only by forcing it down the throats of dissenting teachers and students. But then the same holds for the extreme radical vision.

Antagonistic as they are in most respects, the liberal pluralist and the conservative solutions are actually two sides of the same coin; neither is able to imagine any positive role for cultural conflict. Liberal pluralists are content to let cultural and intellectual diversity proliferate without addressing the conflicts and contradictions that result, whereas conservatives would exclude or shut down those conflicts. Neither strategy works in a world in which cultural and philosophical conflicts, increasingly, can no longer be evaded or shut down. A combination of changing demographic patterns in the wider culture, making student bodies and faculties more diverse, and of unsettling new ideas in the academic disciplines, challenging traditional disciplinary axioms, has created conflicts that cannot be successfully coped with by the traditional educational philosophies and curricular structures, much less by shaking our fists, shouting about relativism and lost standards, and calling for a return to the eternal verities. A solution, however, is latent in the problem itself, if only we can stop listening to those who tell us that controversy is a symptom of barbarism and that education was better in the past because it was calmer.

Where the university *has* failed—and here is the point on which many on the right, left, and center should be able to agree—is in making a focused curriculum out of its lively state of contention. Too much of the current debate is simply irrelevant to the educational problem as it is experienced by the struggling student. The most neglected fact about the culture war is that its issues are clearer and more meaningful to the contending parties than they are to that student. It is not the conflicts dividing the university that should worry us but the fact that students are not playing a more active role in them.

As I argue in Chapters 2 through 6, it won't matter much whose list of books wins the canon debate if students remain disaffected from the life of books and intellectual discussion, as too many have been since long before any canon revisionists arrived on the academic scene. It is easy to forget that for most American students the problem has usually been how to deal with *books* in general, regardless of which faction is drawing up the reading list. Here educators are wasting a major opportunity, for the conflicts that are now adding to the confusions of students have the potential to help them make better sense of their education and their lives. There is really no other choice. These conflicts are not going to go away, and students need to learn to deal with them in the culturally diverse world in which they already live and will live after graduation.

In this book I argue that the best solution to today's conflicts over culture is to teach the conflicts themselves, making them part of our object of study and using them as a new kind of organizing principle to give the curriculum the clarity and focus that almost all sides now agree it lacks. In a sense this solution constitutes a compromise, for it is one that conflicting parties can agree on. But it is really a way of avoiding the evasive compromise represented by the pluralist cafeteria counter curriculum, which leaves it up to students to connect what their teachers do not.

In an important sense, academic institutions are *already* teaching the conflicts every time a student goes from one course or department to another, but they are doing it badly. As I point out in Chapter 6, students typically experience a great clash of values, philosophies, and pedagogical methods among their various professors, but they are denied a view of the interactions and interrelations that give each subject meaning. They are exposed to the *results* of their professors' conflicts but not to the process of discussion and debate they need to see in order to become something more than passive spectators to their education. Students are expected to join an intellectual community that they see only in disconnected glimpses. This is what has passed for "traditional" education, but a curriculum that screens students from the controversies between texts and ideas serves the traditional goals of education as poorly as it serves those of reformers.

Nobody wants to turn the curriculum into a shouting match, of course. But the curriculum is already a shouting match, and one that will only become more angry and polarized if ways are not found to exploit rather than avoid its philosophical differences. When teachers in rival camps do not engage one another in their classrooms, all sides get comfortable preaching to the already converted. We get clashing forms of political correctness that become ever more entrenched the less they are forced to speak to one another. In a vicious circle, opposing viewpoints are so rarely debated that on the rare occasions when they are, the discussion is naturally hostile and confused, and this result then seems to prove that reasoned debate is not possible. Here, as I see it, is the essence of the problems of "Balkanization," separatism, and particularism that have come so to worry us: not the lack of agreement but of the respectful disagreement that supposedly is the strength of democracies and educational institutions.

That is why, however admirable the intention, adding courses in non-Western culture to existing general education requirements (as is now being done or contemplated at many schools and colleges) will only once more postpone the debate that has always been avoided in the past. It is not that non-Western courses are inherently separatist, as so many charge, but that *the established curriculum is separatist,* with each subject and course being an island with little regular connection to other subjects and courses. It is important to bring heretofore excluded cultures into the curriculum, but unless they are put in dialogue with traditional courses, students will continue to struggle with a disconnected curriculum, and suspicion and resentment will continue to increase. For the same reasons, the new field of "cultural studies" should be an open debate about culture and not the euphemism for various kinds of leftist studies that it has become. At the least, cultural studies and women's studies courses should be in dialogue with traditional ones.

In addition to being educationally defective, a disconnected curriculum in which one hand never knows what the other is doing is also very expensive. The cafeteria counter curriculum evolved, after all, during a period of affluence when universities had the luxury to hire specialists in almost everything and encourage them to go their separate ways. Such an ill-coordinated mode of organization would put a commercial firm out of business in a few months, and it may now put many universities out of business if they do not find ways to make teaching more collaborative. I argue in Chapters 6 and 9 that for reasons of both economy and pedagogy we need to rethink what I call the course fetish and the myth of the great teacher, which rest on the notion that by some law of nature teaching must be a solo performance.

I grant that making harsh disagreements productive for education is not easy. How will departments and colleges agree on what to disagree about? Who will determine the agenda of debate and decide which voices are included and excluded, and how will the inequalities between students and teachers, the tenured and the untenured, the eminent and the obscure be overcome? Some will see the introduction of non-Western texts into traditional introductory courses not as a debatable issue but as a capitulation to political pressure. Others will rightly be offended by proposals to debate questions like "Did the Holocaust really happen?" or "Is homosexuality a disease?" where no reputable scholar considers the question open or where it is framed in a way that puts one group on the defensive.

Numerous teachers, departments, and colleges have managed to overcome these obstacles, however, as we shall see in Chapter 9. They have recognized that students need to see the connections between the different interpretations, ideas, and values in the curriculum if they are to enter actively into academic discussions. The point was made best by an instructor who had joined with several colleagues to teach an introductory literature course: "Our students were able to argue with us because they saw us arguing with each other."

These teachers and institutions pick up at the very point at which today's disputes have become deadlocked. They assume that there is something unreal about the either/or choice we have been offered between teaching Western or non-Western culture, that in a culturally diverse society, a wide range of cultures and values should be and will be taught. But they also see that teaching different cultures and values implies teaching them in relation to one another so that the differences and points of intersection become comprehensible. I find it much easier to clarify the traditional idea that great literature is universal when I teach feminist critiques of that idea. Opposing texts and theories need one another to become intelligible to students. As one of my students put it after our class had read Joseph Conrad's *Heart of Darkness* alongside the very different treatment of Africa by the Nigerian novelist Chinua Achebe, *Things Fall Apart,* she thought she better understood the Europeanness of Conrad because she now had something to compare it with (see Chapter 2).

Teaching the conflicts has nothing to do with relativism or denying the existence of truth. The best way to make relativists of students is to expose them to an endless series of different positions which are *not* debated before their eyes. Acknowledging that culture is a debate rather than a monologue does not prevent us from energetically fighting for the truth of our own convictions. On the contrary, when truth is disputed, we can seek it only by entering the debate—as Socrates knew when he taught the conflicts two millennia ago.

Chapter 2

The Vanishing Classics and Other Myths: Two Episodes in the Culture War

W HAT follows are two episodes in the culture war over the university. The first exemplifies the distorted way recent changes in the university are seen from the outside; the second suggests how these changes are experienced from the inside, from the perspective of one teacher's classroom. As we will see, there is a certain discrepancy.

"To Hell with Shakespeare," or the Great *Color Purple* Hoax

THE story that the classics of Western civilization are disappearing from college reading lists has been told so often and so widely that it has virtually become a commonplace of the current educational debate. A recent book reviewer in the *Chicago Tribune*, for example, writes of how "authors central to the western literary and philosophical traditions" are being "stripped from the curriculum and replaced by vociferous enemies of our common culture."[1] The reviewer cites no evidence that what he describes is, in fact, taking place. He obviously thinks he does not have to; that the classics are going out is presumably as obvious as that tuition fees are going up.

Dinesh D'Souza, in his recent best seller *Illiberal Education* asks, "Why are universities expelling Homer, Aristotle, Shakespeare, and other 'white males' from their required reading list?"[2] Again, the way the question is put takes it as established that the state of affairs being described actually exists. The issue is not whether "white males" are, in fact, being "expelled" from required courses, but why. We will see the kind of evidence on which D'Souza bases his observation.

As it happens, the claim that the classics have been or are in the process of being "expelled" and "stripped from the curriculum" is provably false, as D'Souza and the *Tribune* reviewer might have suspected had they taken the trouble to spend a few minutes in the textbook departments of a few campus bookstores. No doubt the full story will someday be told of how the myth of the vanishing classics could have come to be so uncritically believed and disseminated. For now, however, a look at an exemplary case should tell us a good deal.

Early in 1988 Christopher Clausen, head of the English department at Pennsylvania State University, published an article in the *Chronicle of Higher Education* entitled "It Is Not Elitist to Place Major Literature at the Center of the English Curriculum." The article rehearsed what was already by then becoming a familiar set of charges about the damaging effects of canon revisionism on the college curriculum. What was to make Clausen's article memorable, it turned out, was a comment he dropped almost in passing: Clausen observed that he would be willing to "bet that [Alice Walker's] *The Color Purple* is taught in more English courses today than all of Shakespeare's plays combined."[3]

The alarm that the traditional canon was being tossed out had been loudly sounded in 1984 by William J. Bennett, soon to become secretary of education, in a National Endowment for the

Humanities report entitled "To Reclaim a Legacy,"[4] and it was sounded again three years later by Allan Bloom in his best seller *The Closing of the American Mind.*[5] By 1988 reports were circulating about a controversy at Stanford University over its Western civilization course, as Bennett and others charged that the great books were being sacrificed at Stanford to a minority political agenda, subsequently to be labeled "political correctness." Only days before Clausen's article appeared in print, both the *New York Times* and the *Washington Post* had run editorials on the theme of the vanishing classics. In the *Post* article Jonathan Yardley wrote as follows:

> [A]ccording to [current] vigilantes of the English departments, literary quality is irrelevant. . . . Makes you want to rush right back to college, doesn't it? To hell with Shakespeare and Milton, Emerson and Faulkner! Let's boogie! Let's take courses in the writers who really matter, the writers whom the WASPish old guard sneers at. Let's get relevant with courses on Gothic novels, boddice-ripper romances, westerns, detective stories—all of which, The Times advises us, "are proliferating" in the English departments.[6]

As shocking as Yardley's comments were, however, they left vague the actual extent of the damage. No one had reduced it to cold, hard numbers until Clausen offered to wager that Walker's novel had achieved parity with "all of Shakespeare's plays combined."

Nor was it any mere outsider talking now, but the head of one of the nation's major English departments. When someone so close to the scene and in a position of such authority makes such a pronouncement, any reporter or other nonacademic is justified in assuming that he must know what he is talking about. And Clausen would not be the only well-placed professor to declare that the situation was desperate.

It is possible that Clausen imagined his article would be read mostly by fellow academics, who would know enough to discount his improbable estimate as a case of facetious professorial exaggeration. But before anyone could determine whether Clausen was serious, much less take him up on his bet, his *Color Purple* remark had become Exhibit A in a trumped-up charge of canonicide in the national press.

Within days of its publication Clausen's remark was quoted in a fresh denunciation of the canon revisionists in the *Wall Street Journal*. In this article, entitled "From Western Lit to Westerns as Lit," journalist David Brooks gave the strong impression that at Duke University and other campuses, popular authors like Louis L'Amour, "Zane Grey novels, movies and even comic books . . ." had virtually superseded Shakespeare and other classic authors.[7]

The following week Secretary Bennett cited Brooks's *Wall Street Journal* article in a widely reported address in which (as the *Chronicle* reported) he charged that colleges "are eliminating classic works from the curriculum and replacing them with 'nonsense' promoted by 'trendy lightweights.' " The *Chronicle* reporter quoted Clausen's *Color Purple* remark, though without saying if Bennett had referred to it.[8]

A few months later Clausen's *Color Purple* remark and Brooks's *Wall Street Journal* editorial (which had quoted Clausen's remark) were adduced once again in an essay entitled "The Canon under Siege" in the neoconservative *New Criterion*. The fiction writer and man of letters Mark Helprin quoted Clausen and Brooks to back up his claim that literature departments were being taken over by "urban guerillas," who "are not really interested in literature at all" and view it merely "as a tool of oppression (or, at best, a weapon against it), rather than an impartial phenomenon that addresses essential questions beyond and apart from politics."[9] Shortly before Helprin's article, Terry Teachout in *Commentary* had declared that it was the expressed objective of the revisionists "to erase the values of Western culture from the minds of the young by deliberately failing to introduce them to the history and literature in which those values are embodied."[10] Somehow, Teachout neglected to quote Clausen. But by now it was ceasing to matter who was quoting whom.

Clearly a certain picture of reality was forming out of the sheer repetition of the same recycled "evidence" from one over-heated account to the next. The next writer to reinforce the picture was Lynne V. Cheney, Bennett's successor as chairman of the National Endowment for the Humanities. Cheney wrote in *Humanities in America,* a report on the state of the humanities "to the President, the Congress, and the American People," that "viewing humanities texts as though they were primarily political documents is the most noticeable trend in the academic study of the humanities today. Truth and beauty and excellence are regarded as irrelevant," and "questions of intellectual and aesthetic quality" are dismissed.[11] Among the handful of sources for her observation that Cheney cited was Brooks's *Wall Street Journal* article.

All this took place within a few months in 1988. Since then I have seen Clausen's *Color Purple* comment quoted again and again as if it were sober truth. It would take considerable research to track down all these citations, which would be tedious to list in any case, but one of them especially deserves mention: Dinesh D'Souza uses Clausen's comment to nail down the above-mentioned assertion in *Illiberal Education* that universities are "expelling Homer, Aristotle, Shakespeare, and other 'white males' from their required reading list." D'Souza acknowledges that "most colleges still retain a mixture of Western classics and newly introduced texts reflecting the new minority agenda." But the acknowledgment is followed immediately by a warning that the classics' days are numbered. "[T]he late arrivals," writes D'Souza, "are displacing their predecessors as the campaign for curricular diversity gains momentum." D'Souza's evidence? "Perhaps Christopher Clausen, chairman of the English department at Penn State University, reflected the emerging consensus when he remarked, 'I would bet that Alice Walker's *The Color Purple* is taught in more English courses today than all of Shakespeare's plays combined.' "[12]

Did Clausen, D'Souza, or any of the other critics who popularized the *Color Purple* story make any effort to check its accuracy? One might have expected them to, since another part of their complaint was that the very idea of truth was being held in contempt by canon revisionists, who allegedly reduced all knowledge to ideological bias. In fact, it is not difficult to obtain information about the texts being taught in college courses. Most departments now issue course description pamphlets listing the titles and authors to be assigned in the coming semester.

Using such materials myself along with enrollment statistics, I was able in a few hours to make a rough canvass of the texts taught in the Northwestern University English department from the fall of 1986, when Alice Walker's novel was first assigned in a course, to the spring of 1990. Over this four-year period I located two courses in which *The Color Purple* was taught, while I found eight courses that required at least six plays by Shakespeare and eight that required at least two. Shakespeare's dominance became even more visibly one-sided when I totaled the number of students in these courses. The courses assigning at least six Shakespearean plays enrolled 681 students, while the ones assigning at least two enrolled 874, for a total of 1,555 students reading a minimum of two plays. The enrollment in the two courses assigning *The Color Purple* was 124. Thus for every student who read *The Color Purple* 12.5 read at least two of Shakespeare's plays and 5.5 read six or more. In other words, for every reading of Walker there were approximately *eighty-three* readings of Shakespeare. Shakespeare 83, Walker 1.

There is no reason to think Northwestern is exceptional. According to Duke University Professor Cathy Davidson, the Duke English department, "ostensibly the worst offender at tossing out the classics," requires "a 'Major Writers' course on Chaucer, Shakespeare, Milton, and Pope. (Pope!)"[13] None of the exposés on Duke had mentioned this evidently unnewsworthy fact, as none had mentioned that traditional literary approaches are at least as well represented on the Duke literature faculty as recent innovations.

At Stanford also, the extent of curricular change turns out to have been wildly inflated by the critics. D'Souza in his chapter on Stanford draws a scandalous picture in which Plato, Locke, and other canonical figures have given way at Stanford to the likes of Frantz Fanon's *The Wretched of the Earth*. But as John Searle points out in a *New York Review of Books* article that is itself harshly critical of canon revisionism, the revised Stanford program still demands that courses satisfying the humanities requirement assign "the Bible, 'a classical Greek philosopher, an early Christian thinker, a Renaissance dramatist, an Enlightenment thinker,' and readings from Marx and Freud. At least one non-European work must be studied and at some point in each academic quarter 'substantial attention' must be given to 'the issues of *race, gender, and class.*' " Searle judges that only one of the eight courses fulfilling the requirement, a course entitled "Europe and the Americas," represents "a genuinely radical change from the earlier program." And even in this course texts from "the European canon remain, but they are read along with works of Spanish-American, American-Indian, and African-American authors."[14] Searle concludes that the Stanford "controversy became so fogged by political polemics and by partial and inaccurate reports in the press that the cultural issues, and what actually occurred, were not made clear to the general public." In short, "reports of the demise of 'culture,' Western or otherwise, in the required freshman course at Stanford are grossly exaggerated."[15]

More systematically gathered information about the national picture has been available since 1986, thanks to a Modern Language Association (MLA) sampling of catalog descriptions of eighty-one English programs at four-year colleges and universities in 1984–85. According to a report on the sampling, "the basic configuration of the English major appears to have changed only slightly since 1965–68," the period of an earlier study. Most departments (76 percent) still require "historical coverage. . . ."[16] A more comprehensive MLA study of the English major in 271 departments in 1984–85 reveals a similar emphasis on tradition. "Arranged in their approximate descending order of frequency, the courses most commonly prescribed for the major are British literature survey; American literature survey; Shakespeare; history of the English language, linguistics or comparative grammar; and literary criticism or theory."[17]

The MLA study of course catalogs also indicates that though "new courses—in women and literature, black American literature, popular literature, literary theory—have been added to the general English curriculum, . . . few have found their way into the requirements for the major."[18] The key phrase here is "added to"; the most striking changes have been at the edges of the curriculum, in the elective courses, where new texts and topics have been overlaid without altering the shape of the curriculum as a whole or the bread-and-butter requirements, which remain dominated almost as much as they were a half century ago by the likes of Shakespeare, Austen, and Dickens. The Alice Walkers, Toni Morrisons, and Zora Neale Hurstons crop up frequently, but they appear usually as add-ons rather than permanent replacements for the older authors.

This pattern is confirmed by a 1990 MLA survey of texts taught in several upper-division literature courses (i.e., American literature, 1800–1865; the nineteenth-century British novel, preferably the Victorian; and Renaissance literature, excluding Shakespeare). Though the survey was restricted to three courses, its results are nonetheless significant, in part because almost six hundred English faculty members provided information on their courses. According to Phyllis Franklin and her colleagues at the MLA, the findings for nineteenth-century American literature indicate that "respondents give priority to authors who have long been regarded as major figures of the period"—specifically, Hawthorne, Thoreau, Melville, and Emerson. "A similar pattern exists in courses in the British novel. Major writers of the period—

Jane Austen, Charlotte and Emily Brontë, Charles Dickens, George Eliot, Thomas Hardy, and William Makepeace Thackeray—are still being taught and are regarded as important."[19]

Even more to the point than the strong showing of the canonical favorites is the weak one made by their recent challengers. Among authors and works recently added to required readings in nineteenth-century American literature, Harriet Beecher Stowe was the most frequently mentioned noncanonical author. Yet Stowe was listed by only 15 percent of the teachers surveyed. Native American literature has lately been added to required readings by an even more meager 6 percent.[20]

In short, the college literary canon has been changing, as it had for a century, by accretion at the margins, not by dumping the classics. Indeed, no recent revision in the canon has been nearly as abrupt and dramatic as the one that occurred at the end of the nineteenth century, when—in the face of dire predictions by traditionalists that anticipated those of today—the Greek and Latin classics were replaced by English works, which now acquired the title of "the classics."

The state of literature offerings in American high schools is not significantly different from that of the colleges, according to another recent report, by the Center for the Learning and Teaching of Literature at the State University of New York at Albany. The Albany report, written under the chairmanship of the distinguished educational historian Arthur N. Applebee, concludes that as of 1989, "the lists of most frequently required books and authors" are still "dominated by white males, with little change in overall balance from similar lists 25 to 80 years ago." It finds that such figures as Shakespeare, Steinbeck, Dickens, and Twain remain central and that the addition of minority writers seems "to be limited to the margins of the established canon. . . ." The new additions "certainly do not reflect any wholesale rethinking." In fact, in many schools, "there is no evidence of a broadening of the canon to represent a wider spectrum of authors."[21]

My point in producing statistics is not to minimize the changes that have been taking place in the teaching of the humanities, changes we will soon examine more closely. The exposés of political correctness have exaggerated and misrepresented the phenomenon, but they have not made it up. There are those who disregard the norms of democratic debate and seek to turn the entire curriculum into an extension of a radical social agenda, with compulsory reeducation workshops thoughtfully provided for the unenlightened. There are those who justify turning their courses into consciousness raising sessions on the ground that all teaching is inevitably political anyway. This authoritarian behavior is indeed disturbing, and it has been making enemies out of potential friends of the reform movement. But this is hardly an excuse for the critics' apocalyptic descriptions of the entire scene, to whose complications they are oblivious. To put it simply, the critics have not been telling the truth.

Teaching the Politics of *Heart of Darkness*

SINCE I started teaching in the mid-1960s, a work I have assigned frequently is Joseph Conrad's classic *Heart of Darkness,* published in 1899. When I first assigned the novella in 1966 or 1967, I taught it in much the way it had been taught to me in college in the late 1950s, as a profound meditation on a universal moral theme. I presented Conrad's story of the destruction of the idealistic trader Mr. Kurtz as a universal parable of the precarious status of civilized reason in a world overly confident of its having outgrown the primitive and the irrational.

My reading of *Heart of Darkness* as a universal parable of reason and unreason pointed up something in the novel that I still think is important. But this reading also depended on my not seeing certain things or not treating them as worth thinking about. Of little interest to me were the facts that Conrad sets his novella in the Congo in the high period of European colonialism and that he chooses subjugated black Africans to represent the primitive, irrational forces that are Mr. Kurtz's undoing. Conrad, after all, could have chosen any number of ways to symbolize the forces of primitive unreason. That he happened to choose black Africa seemed incidental to his main intention, which was to make a statement about the human condition that would transcend mere questions of nationality and race.

Like Mark Helprin, whom I quoted above from The *New Criterion,* I had been trained to believe that literature is "an impartial phenomenon that addresses essential questions beyond and apart from politics," and I assumed that these transcendent concerns were what the teaching of literature is all about. The subjugation of black Africans was the sort of thing that might interest historians, sociologists, and political scientists, but if the job was to treat literature *as* literature, it was at best of ancillary interest. After all, if God had wanted us to raise political questions in teaching literature, why had he put the departments of English and sociology in separate buildings?

It never occurred to me to ask how a black person might read the story, and the fact that only a small number of black students appeared in my classes helped assure that the question did not come up. Had it come up, however, I would have found it beside the point. What difference did it make who you were and what your history was when you read a literary work? The point of studying literature was to rise above those traces of your upbringing and history. It was Conrad and his vision that mattered, and reflecting on the position from which you read Conrad could only distract attention from his vision to your own narcissistic special interests.

Today I teach *Heart of Darkness* very differently. One critical work that caused me to change my approach was an essay by the Nigerian novelist Chinua Achebe, entitled "An Image of Africa:

Racism in Conrad's *Heart of Darkness*."[22] Achebe argues that Conrad's presentation of black Africa is thoroughly racist. And he is able to accumulate a painfully large number of quotations from both the novel and Conrad's letters and diaries that do reveal how cruelly stereotyped Conrad's thinking about the black African is. Here, for example, is a part of one of the passages quoted by Achebe in which Conrad's narrator, Charlie Marlow, reflects on the position of himself and his shipmates:

> We were wanderers on a prehistoric earth, on an earth that wore the aspect of an unknown planet. We could have fancied ourselves the first of men taking possession of an accursed inheritance, to be subdued at the cost of profound anguish and of excessive toil. But suddenly as we struggled round a bend there would be a glimpse of rush walls, of peaked grass-roofs, a burst of yells, a whirl of black limbs, a mass of hands clapping, of feet stamping, of bodies swaying, of eyes rolling under the droop of heavy and motionless foliage. The steamer toiled along slowly on the edge of a black and incomprehensible frenzy. The prehistoric man was cursing us, praying to us, welcoming us—who could tell? . . . .[23]

Achebe observes that in this passage and often elsewhere in the novel black Africans appear as an undifferentiated mass of eye-rolling, tomtom-beating savages, "a black and incomprehensible frenzy" representing a primitive and "prehistoric" stage of humanity. One is a bit startled to realize that passages of apparent eloquence that have sent chills down the spine of Western readers sound worse than comic when read from Achebe's point of view (though Achebe notes that F. R. Leavis also found the prose of this novel comically bathetic).[24]

Achebe acknowledges that Conrad expresses compassion for the exploited Africans and that he "condemn[s] the evil of imperial exploitation."[25] Yet Achebe argues that ultimately Conrad reduces Africa to a mere "foil for Europe," a mere "setting and backdrop which eliminates the African as human factor," and directs the reader's attention instead to the tragedy of the white imperialist Kurtz. More important and disturbing for Achebe than Conrad's stereotyped portrayal of black Africans is his unspoken assumption about whose point of view counts. As Achebe puts it, "Can nobody see the preposterous and perverse arrogance in thus reducing Africa to the role of props for the break-up of one petty European mind?"[26]

In short, according to Achebe, what Conrad does to black Africa at the level of representation is something like what European imperialism was doing to it. Even in the process of satirizing European imperialism, Conrad uses Africa as a "backdrop" for the implied superiority of European civilization. The real question, Achebe says, "is the dehumanization of Africa and Africans which this age-long attitude has fostered and continues to foster in the world. And the question is whether a novel which celebrates this dehumanization, which depersonalizes a portion of the human race, can be called a great work of art. My answer is: No, it cannot."[27]

I suspect it would be hard for anyone of whatever political persuasion to read Achebe's essay and still read and teach *Heart of Darkness* in quite the same way he or she did before. I at least found I could not. It was not that Achebe's essay convinced me that *Heart of Darkness* is completely racist; in fact, it did not. What Achebe did convince me was that Conrad's assumptions about race are not, as I had imagined, simply an extraneous or nonliterary element of the novel but something that the novel's literary and aesthetic effect depends upon. It had obviously been far easier for me to suspend disbelief in Conrad's assumptions about race and to turn the story into a purely aesthetic experience than it was for Achebe, for whom the way a novel represents black Africans could be truly a matter of life and death.

Then, too, black and third world students were beginning to show up more frequently in my university and my classes—still in pitiful proportions, to be sure, but enough to make it harder for me to take for granted that Conrad's outlook and my own were the natural and normal one. This is not to say that how we read is determined by our color (or gender or ethnic origin). But it would be foolish to deny that the social composition of the students sitting in front of you has an influence on the way you teach. If it did not, we all would still be teaching Greek and Latin instead of English and American literature.

Even if Achebe's interpretation of Conrad is unfair, as I think it is, it forced me to rethink my assumptions about art and politics. For according to Achebe, Conrad's novel is not simply a disinterested work of art, but a text that played and may still be playing an active role in constructing the Western image of black Africa. "Conrad did not originate the image of Africa which we find in his book," Achebe writes. "It was and is the dominant image of Africa in the Western imagination and Conrad merely brought the peculiar gifts of his own mind to bear on it. For reasons which can certainly use close psychological inquiry the West seems to suffer deep anxieties about the precariousness of its civilization and to have a need for constant reassurance by comparison with Africa."[28] Achebe's point is one that recent literary and cultural "theory" has been making, though I think with more complications and qualifications: that literary representations are not simply neutral aesthetic descriptions but interventions that act upon the world they describe. This, in fact, is the point underlying many recent critiques of the idea of *objectivity*, critiques that are poorly understood by their critics; the point is not that there is no truth but that descriptions influence the situations they describe, thereby complicating the problem of truth.

In short, I was forced to rethink not just my interpretation of *Heart of Darkness* but my theoretical assumptions about literature. First, I was forced to recognize that I *had* theoretical assumptions. I had previously thought I was simply teaching the truth about *Heart of Darkness,* "the text itself." I now had to recognize that I had been teaching an interpretation of the text, one that was shaped by a certain *theory* that told me what was and was not worth noticing and emphasizing in my classroom. I had been unable to see my theory *as* a theory because I was living so comfortably inside it.

When I teach *Heart of Darkness* now, as I have in several undergraduate courses for the last few years, I assign Achebe's essay. I do not simply teach Achebe's interpretation as the correct one, however, but ask my students to weigh it against other interpretations. Nor do I discard my earlier reading of the novel as a contemplation of universal truths about the human soul. I assign another critical essay that argues for that interpretation. I also assign several essays (all these materials are included in the Norton Critical Edition of Conrad's novel) by critics who take issue with Achebe. These critics—and I agree with them—grant Achebe's thesis up to a point about Conrad's racism and colonialism but argue that Achebe ignores or minimizes the powerful critique of racism and colonialism that coexists in the novel with these more sinister attitudes.

After Conrad my class reads Achebe's novel *Things Fall Apart,* which presents a counterview of Africa to Conrad's, as if Achebe were trying to wrest the power to represent Africa away from the great European. I supplement these materials with short essays representing opposing sides in the past and present debate over the place, or nonplace, of politics in the arts, illustrating the fact that the debate has a long history dating back to Plato's founding of the history of criticism in an act of political correctness, his expulsion of the poets from his republic for corrupting the morals of the state. Also included in the reading list are several recent neoconservative polemics, some of which say unflattering things about me, impressing my students that their instructor has been abused by so many prominent people. I also invite conservative colleagues into my class to debate the issues with me and my students. To make sure my students enter the debate rather than watch passively from the sidelines, I assign a paper on it or ask them to prepare class presentations in which they give their views.

In short, I now teach *Heart of Darkness* as part of a critical debate about how to read it, which in turn is part of a larger theoretical debate about how politics and power affect the way we read literature. Without claiming to be neutral or disguising my own leanings, I try to help students adjudicate between competing arguments and make informed choices on the key points of contention: Is literature a realm of universal experience that transcends politics, or is it inevitably political, and in what sense of "political," a word too often brandished today without being defined?

I also raise the question of the extent to which a work like *Heart of Darkness* is itself a conflict of theories. Contrary to their opponents, the point of current politically oriented theorists is not that literary works are simple expressions of racism or colonialism but that literature is an arena of conflicting and contradictory social values, a struggle of utopian and dystopian visions.[29] The point needs underscoring: The dominant trend in contemporary theory is *not* to reduce literary works to transparent expressions of ideology, whether for good or bad. This is the impression that has been presented by critics whose dislike of recent theory exceeds their willingness to read it. The most powerful and influential of recent theories argue that literature is a scene of contradictions that cannot be subsumed under any "totalizing" ideology.

The only prominent critic of theory I know who gets this right is Frederick Crews of the University of California at Berkeley. As Crews concisely and accurately sums it up, the primary message of recent theory is "that literature is a site of struggle whose primary conflicts, both intrapsychic and social, deserve to be brought to light rather than homogenized into notions of fixed authorial 'values.' "[30] Crews has provided what seems to me a model of what a scrupulous critique of current theory would look like: He shows how at its worst this kind of theory simply replaces the clichés and predictable readings of earlier critical schools with a new set of clichés and predictable readings, but how at its best it has revitalized whole fields such as Faulkner studies.

Far from debasing the academic standards of my courses, teaching *Heart of Darkness* as I now teach it seems to me to have made my courses considerably *more* challenging than they were previously. For my students now have to be more reflective about their assumptions than they had to be before, and they are now asked to take part in a set of complex debates that I previously did not expect them to. Nor, I think, do the critical and theoretical debates I teach distract students from the close reading of literary works in themselves. When it seemed to me at one point that my students were agreeing too easily with Achebe, I corrected by restating the aesthetic reading of *Heart of Darkness* and the need to return constantly to the verbal particulars of the text.

In the end I think Achebe's critique pushes my students to a closer reading of the verbal and stylistic particularity of *Heart of Darkness* than they would achieve through an exclusively aesthetic approach. Then, too, I think it also enables them to understand more clearly just what an "aesthetic approach" is, since they now have something to compare it with. Before, students would look blank when I used words like "aesthetic" (or "traditional," "humanistic," etc.), as if to say, " 'Aesthetic' as opposed to *what?*" Introducing a challenge to traditional values helps students understand what is at stake in embracing or rejecting them.

Was I really being less "political" when I taught *Heart of Darkness* without mentioning the issue of race than I am now when I put that issue in the foreground? In today's climate of hysterical accusation and denunciation, merely to raise the question for debate is for some of us enough to convict a teacher of the crime of political correctness. Yet it seems to me reasonable to argue that something political is at stake in whose representation of black Africa, Conrad's or Achebe's, gets into the debate, just as something political is at stake in whether other representations of the culture war get into the national media besides the ones favored by those who see nothing on the scene but the takeover of "urban guerillas."

The way of teaching I have described will obviously not recommend itself to all teachers. Not all teachers will be comfortable dealing with political conflicts, nor is there any reason why they should have to. I choose to deal with these political conflicts not because I take them to be the only ones worth teaching but because they do have a good deal of urgency in our culture today and because I think frank discussion of these conflicts is more likely to improve our handling of them than pretending they do not exist.

In this, I like to think I am moving toward a solution to the current controversies that other teachers are also finding today, which is to incorporate the controversies themselves into my reading list and course framework. Instead of choosing between the Western Conrad and the non-Western Achebe, I teach the conflict between their novels and between competing views of literature.

One dividend of this approach I did not expect. Teaching *Things Fall Apart,* I found the novel not only first-rate literature and a source of insight into a culture unfamiliar to me but a means of illuminating *Heart of Darkness* that I had not previously had. When I had taught Conrad's novel as a universal statement, my students seemed to find the concept of universality difficult and elusive—or perhaps they simply could not see the point of insisting on it. Again, "Universality as opposed to what?" seemed to be their unspoken thought. Once I introduced Achebe, however, with his sharp challenge to the idea that Conrad's world view is the universal one, the concept of universality came into much clearer focus for my students. The "Western" aspect of Conrad suddenly became a less mystifying quality now that students had something to contrast it with. And this led in turn to the question of whether "Western" and "non-Western" are really mutually exclusive.

"I Better Watch My Grammar"

IF the flagrant misrepresentation typified by the *Color Purple* case erases the reality of how the humanities are actually being taught today, the reasons for the misrepresentation can only partly be attributed to the organized power of the right over certain sectors of the media. Part of the problem lies also in the peculiar difficulty of representing intellectual developments in the press. A vulgarized version of a theory or critical approach is inevitably easier to describe in the confines of a brief news article than the best, most sophisticated version of the theory or approach. A doctrinaire assault on "dead white males" can be easily summarized in a column inch or two, whereas it would take many pages to describe intellectual movements that are complex, diverse, and rife with internal conflicts. Glib falsifications can always be produced at a faster rate than their refutations.

Then, too, few readers of the popular press are in a position to recognize misrepresentations of academic practices, a fact that relieves anyone who wants to debunk these practices of the responsibility to do their homework. So feminism, multiculturalism, and deconstructionism are understood not as a complicated and internally conflicted set of inquiries and arguments about the cultural role of gender, ethnicity, language, and thought but as a monolithic doctrine that insists, as D'Souza formulates it, "that texts be selected primarily or exclusively according to the author's race, gender, or sexual preference and that the Western tradition be exposed in the classroom as hopelessly bigoted and oppressive in every way."[31] Such views may characterize a Leonard Jeffries, the City College of New York Professor whose absurd speculations about "ice people" (Europeans) and "sun people" (Africans) have indeed had a lamentable influence on certain Afrocentric school curricula. But anyone who takes these views to be typical of academic revisionist thinking simply knows nothing of the reality.

I do not deny that others can be found who hold these disturbingly crude doctrines and that some of them see nothing wrong with forcing them on others. But no academic critic of any standing or influence does not repudiate these doctrines, and it is unfair to judge any trend by its least admirable versions. This caricaturing practice has obscured the fact that virtually every major advance in humanistic scholarship over the last three decades is indebted to the movements that are widely accused of subverting scholarly values: feminism, ethnic studies, postcolonialism, deconstruction, and the new historicism. The irony is that these movements have themselves been so concerned about challenging naïve notions of disinterested objectivity that they have failed to emphasize their own objective contribution to our knowledge. The conservatives, on the other hand, who defend scholarly values against politics, have produced little humanities scholarship of interest but a great many political polemics.

There is still another reason why myths about the academy have flourished, however, and this is one for which the academy has itself to blame. Academics have given journalists and others little help in understanding the more difficult forms of academic work. As this work has become increasingly complex and as it increasingly challenges conventionally accepted forms of thinking, the university acquires an obligation to do a more effective job of popularization. Yet the university has been disastrously inept in this crucial popularizing task and often disdains it as beneath its dignity. If the university has become easy prey for ignorant or malicious misrepresentations, it has asked for them. Having treated mere image making as beneath its dignity, the academy has left it to its detractors to construct its public image for it.

Until recently it has been a common joke among English professors that when people meet one of our species at a party, all they can think to say is, "Oh, you teach English? I guess I better watch my grammar." It would not have been so easy to replace this older image of the English professor as a grammatical pedant with the new image of "urban guerilla" had the discipline thought more seriously about clarifying its concerns to outsiders. This would mean not simply speaking more clearly, however, but also respecting the objections of those whose minds one presumably hopes to change.

This is where the argument of this book comes in: I argue that the poor quality of communication between the academic humanities and the outside world has a lot to do with the poor quality of communication between academic humanists themselves and between sectors of the university in general. If the university is poor at representing itself to the wider student body and the public, the problem lies not just in its notorious proclivity for jargon. It has a deeper source in institutional practices that isolate teachers from one another and prevent conflicting views from entering into clarifying dialogues. In the absence of continuous public discussion and debate, doctrines harden and paranoid myths proliferate—like the myth that *The Color Purple* is replacing Shakespeare or that new academic theories are attempts to destroy Western civilization. By changing these institutional practices, we can clarify the real controversies in the academy and dispel the myths surrounding them.

Chapter 3

How to Save
"Dover Beach"

THE scene: the English department faculty lounge at Middle America University. An older professor enters, draws a cup of coffee, and remarks that he has just come from teaching Matthew Arnold's famous Victorian poem "Dover Beach" and was appalled to discover that his students found the poem virtually incomprehensible. Here is another sorry illustration, he sighs wearily, of the deplorably ill-prepared state of our students today. Why—can you believe it?—says the older male professor (I'll call him OMP for short), these students hardly knew what to make of the famous concluding lines, which he recites with slightly self-mocking grandiloquence:

> Ah, love, let us be true
> To one another! for the world, which seems
> To lie before us like a land of dreams,
> So various, so beautiful, so new,
> Hath really neither joy, nor love, nor light,
> Nor certitude, nor peace, nor help for pain;
> And we are here as on a darkling plain

Swept with confused alarms of struggle and flight,
Where ignorant armies clash by night.[1]

One of his colleagues who happens to be in the lounge, a young woman who teaches courses in literature by women (let's call her YFP), replies that she can appreciate the students' reaction. She recalls that being forced to study "Dover Beach" in high school caused her to form a dislike for poetry that it had taken her years to overcome.

OMP (furiously stirring his Coffee-mate): In *my* humble opinion—reactionary though I suppose it now is—"Dover Beach" is one of the great masterpieces of the Western tradition, a work that, until recently at least, every seriously educated person took for granted as part of the cultural heritage.

YFP: Perhaps, but is that altogether to the credit of the cultural heritage? Take those lines addressed to the woman: "Ah, love, let us be true to one another . . ." and so forth. In other words, protect and console me, my dear—as it's the function of your naturally more spiritual sex to do—from the "struggle and flight" of politics and history that we men have been assigned the regrettable duty of dealing with. It's a good example of how women have been defined by our culture as naturally private and domestic and therefore justly disqualified from sharing male power.

OMP: So much for teaching "Dover Beach," then . . .

YFP: On the contrary, we *should* teach "Dover Beach." But we should teach it as the example of phallocentric discourse that it is.

OMP: That's the trouble with you people; you seem to treat "Dover Beach" as if it were a piece of political propaganda rather than a work of art. To take Arnold's poem as if it were an instance of "phallocentric discourse," whatever that is, misses the whole point of poetry, which is to rise above such transitory issues by transmuting them into universal human experience. To read poems as if they were statements about gender politics replaces the universal concerns of art with the gripes of a special-interest group. "Dover Beach" is no more about gender politics than *Macbeth* is about the Stuart monarchical succession.

YFP: But *Macbeth* is about the Stuart monarchical succession, among other things—or at least its original audience may well have thought so. It's about gender politics, too: Why does Lady Macbeth have to "unsex" herself to qualify to commit murder? Not to mention the business about men born of woman and from their mothers' womb untimely ripped. It's not that "Dover Beach" and *Macbeth* are "statements about gender politics" but that these texts assume definitions of men's and women's "natures" that still shape our behavior and that we blind ourselves to if we read them as accounts of universal experience.

What you take to be the universal human experience in Arnold and Shakespeare, Professor OMP, is male experience presented as if it were universal. You don't notice the presence of politics in literature—or in sexual relations, for that matter—because for you patriarchy is simply the normal state of affairs and therefore as invisible as the air you breathe. My reading of "Dover Beach" seems to you to reflect a "special-interest" agenda, but to me yours does, too. You can afford to "transmute" the sexual politics of literature onto a universal plane, but that's a luxury I don't enjoy.

At this point other colleagues passing through the lounge begin to jump in. An old-fashioned formalist close reader asks YFP where, in "Dover Beach," there is any indication that the speaker and addressee are respectively male and female. Might not Arnold have avoided specifying the genders, he asks, precisely to stress the universal nature of the experience? "Don't you concede that all of us at times, women and men both, have felt fed up with politics as a clash of ignorant armies? Then, too, the mutuality of the experience seems to be stressed—'let *us* be true *to one another*. . . .' It's an equal partnership."

OMP (beaming): Precisely, precisely.

YFP: Honestly now, have you ever encountered anyone who read "Dover Beach" as spoken by a woman to a man? I know I haven't. Could any woman in Victorian England—even Victoria herself—have spoken with such a voice? It's true that the impulse to escape into private experience is felt by everyone, but that's my point. Women are no more naturally "private" than men, but historically that's the role they've been assigned. Because of this difference in our histories, "let us be true to one another" says something different to me from what it says to you. But suppose you're right. Suppose that we read the poem as spoken by a woman to a man (or, for that matter, two people of the same sex) and that the speaker assumes a more equal relation between the parties than I see. This would not make the poem any less political; it would simply make it a *different* politics, a better politics, but still a politics. . . .

Another feminist chimes in, saying, "Yes, I'm glad you acknowledge the possibility of a more complex politics in the poem than a straightforward 'phallocentric discourse.' As you know, feminist criticism long ago moved away from attacking white male authors for sexism. I think most current feminists would see a conflict of attitudes toward love in the poem—on the one hand, a desire for utopian equality between the sexes; on the other, the man doing all the talking and reveling in melo-dramatic self-pity. . . ."

A more up-to-date close reader enters the fray. "If I take that further, it seems to me that both of you, OMP and YFP, are partly right and that something like your conflict remains unre-solved in 'Dover Beach' itself. Arnold *tries* to do what you see it as doing, OMP, to assert the transcendence of love and the great art and religions of the past, which are invoked earlier in the poem, over the 'ignorant armies' of contemporary history and politics. But in recognizing those ignorant armies, he is forced to acknowledge the pull of history and social conflict that chal-lenges the universals he wants to reaffirm. Arnold is not aware of the gender conflicts you're concerned with, YFP (which is your point), but the turbulence of nineteenth-century social upheaval is surely there in the reference to 'struggle and flight. . . .' "

Predictably, this interpretation only provoked further objections. The discussion continued. . . .

Common Culture or Common Debate?

THE scene I have just described is the sort that has been occurring with increasing frequency lately in faculty lounges, department meetings, and academic cocktail parties. It exemplifies— necessarily in overly schematic terms—what today's educational critics have in mind when they charge that the academic humanities have fallen into a state of disarray and confusion. It illustrates their point that shared literary and artistic traditions, commonly agreed-upon standards of value, and the very idea of a common culture are in peril. The argument YFP makes is the kind of which conservative columnist George Will is thinking when he writes of those who are assaulting "the common culture that is the nation's social cement."[2]

Even those who wouldn't necessarily put all the blame on YFP tend to see the conflict as a catastrophe for education. "Is there no way out of this impasse?" asks a cover story on the educational crisis in a national weekly. "Or are we doomed to an endless tug of war over words between the very people who should be leading us onward to a better life?"[3] Another prominent commentator, James Atlas, strikes the same note of desperation:

> If we as a society can't agree that there is a body of knowledge to be mastered, much less what that body is, our very continuance as a literate culture will be in doubt. And that threat exists on all levels, from elementary schools in the slums to graduate seminars in the

Ivy League. Saving our schools isn't just a matter of improving test scores or teaching children to read. There has to be a vision of what it is we wish them to know.[4]

The note is struck again by Arthur Schlesinger, Jr., in *The Disuniting of America: Reflections on a Multicultural Society,* a book which argues that multicultural education is plunging American culture into "incoherence and chaos."[5]

These statements eloquently illustrate the way we are encouraged to think about the crisis of education: Fundamental disagreement over what students should know is an "impasse"; it threatens "our very continuance as a literate culture," spelling "incoherence and chaos." If OMP, YFP, and others equally at odds cannot somehow settle their disputes, then the quality of American education can only deteriorate.

It is true that seemingly more constructive versions of the diagnosis can be found. Former Secretary of Education William J. Bennett declares that we must recover "a clear vision of what is worth knowing and what is important in our heritage that all educated persons should know." He goes on to assure us that "it is a grave error" to base a college curriculum on the assumption "that it is no longer possible to reach a consensus on the most significant thinkers, the most compelling ideas, and the books all students should read. . . . There is more consensus on what the important books are than many people have been willing to admit."[6]

Critics like Bennett have captured a following by the appearance they give of seeing through cowardly professorial evasions and calling us back to educational fundamentals. They seem to say, in effect, "It's time to cut out the nonsense and start facing up to the hard questions. The professors and administrators have lost their nerve; they have caved in to the radicals and the special-interest groups and let the curriculum go to the dogs. We must get back to teaching the things that really matter—and can we seriously doubt that we know what these things are?"

It is Bennett and his fellow critics, however, who are actually dodging all the hard questions. They have no strategy for dealing with cultural and educational conflict except to deny its legitimacy. What really bothers them is that there should *be* a fundamental controversy over the curriculum at all, for they assume that without a consensus all is lost.

Is it, in fact, the case, however, that, as Atlas puts it, "our very continuance as a literate culture" is placed in jeopardy by fundamental disagreement over what should be taught? Is it true that attempts to make the curriculum more representative of the nation's diverse peoples and beliefs must spell curricular incoherence and chaos? Is it true that disputes provoked by teachers like the younger female professor over the relevance of gender questions in teaching poems and novels lower the quality of education?

Nobody could disagree with Bennett that without a "clear vision" of education we are in deep trouble. But it does not at all follow that a clear vision cannot tolerate—indeed, thrive upon—fundamental disagreement about "the most significant thinkers, the most compelling ideas, and the books all students should read. . . ." What Bennett, Schlesinger, Atlas, and others lack is any faith that our disagreements about such questions might be energizing rather than paralyzing.

When one considers the enormous diversity of American universities, it seems strangely self-defeating to think of disagreement as an impasse. For many decades now ambitious universities have been systematically recruiting faculties that would represent the increasing multiplicity of human knowledge and culture. It is this intellectual and cultural richness that has made American higher education the envy of the world. A college president who did *not* find deep conflicts of principle on his or her faculty would have far more reason to worry than one who found such conflicts frequently. A state of peace and quiet would indicate that major perspectives had been excluded, the sure sign of a second-rate institution. Yet having programmed the inevitability of ideological contention into our system, we seem shocked to discover there is so much ideological contention around.

To be sure, there are numerous walks of life in which basic disagreements like the one between OMP and YFP would spell disaster. If half the mechanics in an auto repair shop fall to quarreling with the other half about the very validity of repairing car engines, the shop will have indeed reached an impasse. If the members of a baseball team disagree about the very value of winning ball games, the team is indeed in trouble. But education can thrive on conflicts that would undermine other enterprises because it can make them part of its business. I would not be human if I did not want my students to agree with my interpretations of texts and my views of literature and culture. But I suspect my best courses have been those which helped my students articulately to disagree with me.

We are right to seek a clear vision of what educated people should know, but we have been looking for that vision in the wrong place. We have been seeking it in a consensus that has become increasingly less attainable as American education has become increasingly less culturally and philosophically homogeneous. A really clear vision would see that when what educated persons should know is deeply disputed, the dispute itself becomes part of what educated persons should know. Once the cultural status of "Dover Beach" has become controversial, that controversy becomes part of the study of literature.

Even if Bennett is right that there is more consensus than we recognize on the important thinkers, ideas, and books, deep differences remain in the way these books are interpreted and taught. "Dover Beach" as taught by OMP will seem so different a poem from "Dover Beach" as taught by YFP that it may hardly look like the same work to a student who takes courses from both. For this reason, agreement could be reached tomorrow on a core list of texts and little of the current contention would abate.

Does this mean, then, that the very idea of a common culture must be scrapped? It depends what is meant by that too loosely used term "common culture." What is troubling about those who invoke the idea of common culture against teachers like YFP is their habit of speaking as if the content of that culture were already *settled*—as if there were no question about what the common culture will include and who will have a voice in defining it. When Bennett subtitles a book *Improving America's Schools and Affirming the Common Culture,* he thinks of the common culture as if it were already finished and completed, something that people just "affirm" or don't affirm rather than something people struggle to create through democratic discussion.

Bennett fails to make the crucial distinction between a common culture based on agreement about questions like the meaning and value of "Dover Beach" and a *common discussion* about culture, which implies agreement only to debate our different beliefs, tastes, and values, with the help of whatever common language, assumptions, and conclusions we are able to discover through the process of discussion itself. For there is always a background of agreement that makes disagreement possible, and through debate that area of agreement can be widened. We need to distinguish between a shared body of national beliefs, which democracies can do nicely without, and a common national debate about our many differences, which we now need more than ever.

A famous story has it that Gandhi, on being asked what he thought of Western civilization, replied that in his opinion it would be a very good idea. Gandhi's remark nicely captures what feminists, multiculturalists, and other dissenting academicians have lately been saying about the idea of a common culture: that it would be a very good idea. Even the more separatist elements within these movements—they are more pervasive in the schools than in the colleges—are not rejecting the idea of a common culture so much as asking for a greater voice in defining it. The "multi" in "multiculturalism" denotes the mixing of cultures, not their self-isolation, though this is a complex debate within multiculturalism, as one would never know from its critics.

What most multiculturalists and feminists question is not the ideal of a common culture but the assumption that this ideal is already a realized fact, excusing us to return to educational business as usual after adding a few token minority texts to the syllabus. The quarrel of these groups is not with the idea of shared cultural experience but with the use of that idea as an excuse for inequality and injustice, as if to say, So what if there is a huge and widening gulf in the United States between rich and poor, white and black, majority and minority cultures? We're all part of the common culture, aren't we?

Schlesinger, who attacks multiculturalism for "divisively" encouraging the fragmentation of our own culture "into a quarrelsome spatter of enclaves, ghettos, tribes," argues that "the bonds of cohesion in our society are sufficiently fragile, or so it seems to me, that it makes no sense to strain them by encouraging and exalting cultural and linguistic apartheid."[7] But we won't strengthen fragile "bonds of cohesion" by attacking others for being divisive. As Schlesinger himself concedes, it was not the multiculturalists but a complex and violent history that created the "enclaves, ghettos, [and] tribes" to which he refers. As historian Joan W. Scott points out, when critics like Schlesinger (and C. Vann Woodward) blame multiculturalists for exacerbating divisiveness and difference, they act "as if divisiveness and difference existed only because people called attention to it."[8] To tell those who have been forcibly excluded from the benefits of the melting pot that their complaints are too "divisive" is a good way to drive them into permanent opposition.

The current attack on "divisiveness," "Balkanization," and so forth is really an attack on the unpleasant fact of social conflict itself while fobbing off the responsibility for it on somebody else. It represents an essentially defensive and frightened way of responding to conflict, one that prevents us from seeing that it is precisely in divisive disagreements like that between OMP and YFP that the starting point for a common cultural discussion might be found.

What Is Good for "Dover Beach"?

THAT is all well and good, one may say, but surely such faculty squabbling can only be bad for "Dover Beach," no? Isn't it just like professors to get so enmeshed in their petty professional bickering that they lose sight of both the great texts and their students? Perhaps so, but before answering too quickly in the affirmative, we should stop and ask how well "Dover Beach" was doing in college and high school literature classes before teachers like YFP came along. We need only look at OMP's complaint about his students' ill-preparedness which triggered the lounge debate—and it has been a perennial one among teachers—to recall the many problems students had with such texts long before teachers like YFP arrived on the scene. Classics like "Dover Beach" have often inspired student apathy even when taught in the most reverential way—perhaps especially when taught in the most reverential way.

In fact, in a country where literature has not exactly been high on the list of national priorities, there is something a bit bizarre about the belief that the eruption of a passionate quarrel over literature is bad for it. What would truly be bad for "Dover Beach" is if no such quarrel existed, something that would imply that we do not care enough about such works to bother going to battle over them. The classics, I suggest, have less to fear from newfangled ideological hostility than from old-fashioned indifference.

Was literature really better off before 1965 because exchanges like the one in the faculty lounge did not take place? The 1950s are often presented to us today as the last good time for education, when the literary canon was still intact and presumably

taught without political agendas getting in the way. In a celebrated *New Yorker* essay on T. S. Eliot, Cynthia Ozick writes of
the "exultation" felt toward Eliot by "anyone who was an undergraduate in the forties or the fifties (or possibly even in the first
years of the sixties)." Ozick contrasts that era of earnest literary
passion with "the accelerating disrespect for serious high culture" in the university today. Today, Ozick declares, "high art is
dead. The passion for inheritance is dead. Tradition is equated
with obscurantism. The wall that divided serious high art from
the popular arts is breached; anything can count as 'text.' "[9]

Having been an undergraduate myself in the mid-fifties, I can
only say I don't remember it the way Ozick does. I do recall
teachers and students who treated Eliot and his fellow literary
modernists as sacrosanct, but they could not have been more
than a coterie, and a rather despised one at that. It is true, the
Beat Generation notwithstanding, that there were few expressions of "disrespect" for high culture (if you except the country's
general indifference to it). And it is true that a particular Western canon was intact, though it was hardly lacking in a political
agenda, reflecting as it did the Christian conservatism of Eliot
and his followers. Was this stability, however, a sign that the
classics were sacred or simply that they were taken for granted?
The canon was intact, to be sure, but in a way that did not
glorify literature so much as discourage impolite questions from
being raised about it.

Had I been exposed to a little "disrespect" for the classics, I
might have found studying them more rewarding than I did. I
might have sooner acquired the sort of critical context for
understanding those forbidding texts for which (as I relate in
the following chapter) I groped without success. Had anyone
taught me then that "anything can count as 'text' "—the recent
semiotic theory that Ozick evidently mistakes for a nihilistic lev-
eling of value distinctions—it might have made high culture seem
less frighteningly remote from the popular culture I was com-

fortable with. The point is not to replace Ozick's sentimental stereotype of the fifties with an equally bogus accusatory stereotype. I invoke my recollections only to suggest that accounts like Ozick's have less to do with the real past than with the need to make the present seem corrupt and fallen.*

What has really been disastrous for classics like "Dover Beach" is the belief that we honor such classics by protecting them from disrespect. Though this protective attitude postures as a form of reverence for Western culture, it really betrays a lack of confidence in that culture, whose monuments we evidently fear cannot stand up to criticism. It is Western insecurity, not Western self-confidence, that one senses beneath the chest-thumping exhortations heard today to stop acting like wimps, whiners, and victim lovers and to stand up for the superiority of the West. In fact, the West-Is-Besters are doing precisely what they denounce others for: reveling in self-pity, presenting themselves as helpless victims, and using the curriculum to prop up a flagging self-esteem. Anybody who was really confident of the West's accomplishments would welcome strong criticism of them. When writers like Schlesinger point out that Western culture itself has been profoundly self-critical, they seem not to see that they are making an argument for intensifying that criticism, not desisting from it.

In offering such strong criticism, teachers like YFP are in an odd way doing "Dover Beach" a favor. Even in accusing Arnold's poem of ideological mystification, YFP's critique does more to make the poem *a live issue* in the culture again than does the respectful treatment of traditionalist teachers like OMP, which fails to arouse his students. Paradoxically, it is the defensive attitude toward the classics—treating them as a fragile inheritance

---

* Not fallen and corrupt enough, however, to satisfy world-class connoisseurs. Ozick's essay was denounced by Hilton Kramer for its halfhearted condemnations of the present scene. (See Kramer, "Cynthia Ozick's Farewell to T. S. Eliot—and High Culture," *The New Criterion* 8, no. 6 [February 1990]: 5–9.)

that must be protected from the profane contemporary culture around them—that has often made the classics seem cold, remote, and uninteresting to students, especially those who come in already conditioned to think of book culture as rarefied and irrelevant. The best way to kill the classics has always been to put them on a pedestal, safe from the contemporary forces that challenge them.

Here lies the fallacy in the common charge that teachers like YFP are nihilistically debunking the very concept of literary *value*— as if that concept had been thriving wonderfully before she came on the scene. As long as I can remember, traditionalists have complained that though the university characteristically teaches students how to *analyze* literary works, to take them apart and put them back together in ingenious ways, it utterly fails to teach them how to tell a good poem or novel from a bad one. If this is no longer the case, it is only thanks to the emergence of teachers like YFP, who have restored evaluation to a central position in literary study by pointing out that judgments of what constitutes good and bad art have always been related to judgments about what makes for good and bad societies. As the critic W. J. T. Mitchell observes, movements like feminism, neo-Marxism, the new historicism, and neopragmatism all reflect "a renewed concern for the relation between the professional study of the humanities and issues of public policy, national interest, and cultural identity."[10]

One might think traditionalists would be encouraged by the revival of their own favorite questions about the civic role of the arts, but of course, the new ways of reviving the question of value are not what traditionalists had in mind. Evaluating literature has come to be thought of as a process in which we efface our particular social circumstances and become a kind of neutral everyman. If a work is good, it is good in itself apart from whoever happens to be reading it under whatever circumstances. YFP's argument seems shocking because she rejects this universal contract and refuses to forget who she is and where she came from when she reads "Dover Beach." In asserting that she does not have the luxury to forget she is a woman, YFP says, in effect, that because women have historically been treated differently from men, something different can be at stake for them even in something so seemingly harmless as how a woman is addressed in a love poem. (YFP is not the first to have noticed a certain male pomposity in "Dover Beach"; Anthony Hecht has satirized this very quality in his widely anthologized poem "The Dover Bitch" ["... To have been brought/all the way down from London, and then be addressed/As a sort of mournful cosmic last resort/Is really tough on a girl. . . ."].)[11]

YFP asks OMP to consider that reading "Dover Beach" can legitimately be a different experience for her than for him—just as the anti-Semitism of *The Merchant of Venice* or of Ezra Pound's "Pisan Cantos" is likely to be a different experience for Jews than for non-Jews, or, as we have seen, the portrayal of Africa as a primitive stage of civilization in Joseph Conrad's *Heart of Darkness* is likely to be a different experience for blacks than for whites. (See Chapter 8 for further discussion of this issue.)

YFP is doing a favor not only for "Dover Beach" but for OMP as well. Her challenge to his traditional view of literature gives this view a meaning and potential interest for students that it has hitherto sadly lacked. OMP's students do not respond to studying "Dover Beach" as an expression of "universal human experience" because such pious phrases have little significance in the culture they have grown up in. (The word "universality" is almost as remote from the everyday vocabulary of many students as "deconstruct" or "problematize.") To many of them such traditional language is reminiscent of the sanctimonious teacher talk that caused them from the early grades to decide that literature is boring. Once this traditional language comes under attack by YFP, however, students may see that it is not merely a set of meaningless platitudes but that something important is at stake in whether you embrace or reject it. To some students OMP's defense of universality against YFP may make him seem downright heroic.

We need to rethink the notion that we best serve the humanities by praising them in the very terms that once put generations of students to sleep. This is what National Endowment for the Humanities Chairman Lynne V. Cheney ignores when she repeatedly insists that our emphasis should be on what the humanities tell us about topics like "what it means to be human," what it means "to know joy and find purpose nonetheless; to be capable of wisdom and folly. . . ."[12] If Cheney's threadbare phrases have become interesting again today, it is only because they have been challenged by the likes of YFP. Cheney and OMP need YFP (and vice versa) to make their positions meaningful—or even intelligible—to students who do not come to the university already knowing why the universality of the humanities should need defending.

I am suggesting that what is threatened by the debate in the faculty lounge is not "Dover Beach" but OMP's conception of "Dover Beach" as a repository of universal values that stand above controversy, above politics, above who we are as readers and the different backgrounds and interests we bring to our reading. Whereas this conflict-free idea of culture once held a privileged place in humanistic education as something that went without saying, it has now become one *theory* among others, something that you have to argue for against competing theories. This is what most bothers OMP: that the literary canon, once seen as an accepted heritage to be noiselessly passed from one generation to the next, has become a conflict of theories.

Theory Has Broken Out

ONE way to describe the conflict in the faculty lounge, then, is to say that theory has broken out. "Theory," by my definition anyway, is what erupts when what was once silently agreed to in a community becomes disputed, forcing its members to formulate and defend assumptions that they previously did not even have to be aware of. As soon as OMP and YFP discover they hold conflicting assumptions about poetry in general, they have no choice but to have a dispute about theoretical questions: What is poetry? Should students study it and why, and how should it be taught? How do we know what a poem like "Dover Beach" or a play like *Macbeth* is about?

Teachers like OMP tend to see this kind of discussion as a lamentable diversion of our attention from literary works—as if what we mean by "literature" should not need to be disputed. Others, as we have seen, view it as a case of the professors bickering among themselves and losing sight of their object of study, as if those who make this objection were not implicated in the "bickering." Literature is not being left behind in the dispute between OMP and YFP, however, but rather is being discussed in the more theoretically conscious way that becomes necessary when we no longer agree on the nature and function of literature. As Terry Eagleton argues, "without some kind of theory, however unreflective and implicit, we would not know what a 'literary work' was in the first place, or how we were to read it. Hostility to theory usually means opposition to other people's theories and an oblivion of one's own."[13]

A variant of this objection holds that while theoretical debate is all well and good in its place, in the usual undergraduate teaching situation there isn't time for it. Had we but world enough and time, this objection runs, debates on the politics of poetry like the one engaged in by OMP, YFP, and their colleagues might be valuable to explore. But considering the inevitable constraints, especially with students who may be taking their sole literature class in college, the teacher's primary responsibility must be to teach "Dover Beach" itself. After all, how can undergraduates be expected to fathom such theoretical debates if they cannot yet make out the prose sense of "Dover Beach"—and probably do not even know where Dover Beach is?

I try to show in my next chapter how disastrous for the teaching of literature has been the seemingly commonsensical view that critical and theoretical talk about literature *competes* with reading "literature itself." Suffice it to say here that OMP (or any other teacher) is *already* implicitly teaching his theories when he teaches "Dover Beach." Teaching theory is not a question of *adding* something to one's analysis of the poem itself but of explaining what one is doing and why one is doing it that way and not another. In an important sense OMP and YFP are already teaching their theoretical debate even if they never mention their assumptions to their classes. Teachers who claim there is not enough time for theory remind me of the politician who reportedly asked, "How can you expect me to be concerned about ethics when there are all these other things I have to do?"

I do not deny that much that goes under the name of theory in today's academy is dubious (though I doubt it is any more dubious than second-rate traditional criticism or mediocre literary journalism) and that it often defeats its purpose by being needlessly obscure. The very word "theory" is misleadingly bloodless and off-putting, with its connotations of a specialized, esoteric discourse that is over the head of the layperson. Few who react violently against "theory" would object to the proposition that we inevitably have *general ideas* about such practices as writing and reading or that when disagreement erupts over these practices, it is often necessary and useful to debate our principles. The critics have every right to dislike the *kinds* of "theory" that are popular in today's academy, but to attack theory as such is equivalent to attacking thinking. As Eagleton's above comment implies, "theory" denotes nothing more than *philosophy,* the sort of reflection on our assumptions and practices without which any person or institution goes brain dead.

We do not usually reflect on our assumptions and practices unless something forces us to, however, and what usually provides that stimulus is conflict, some challenge to premises that previously seemed so obvious that we did not have to be aware of them as such. "Theory" is a name for the kind of self-consciousness that results when a community ceases to agree on these heretofore seemingly obvious, "normal" assumptions—like the assumption that women are domestic by nature, or that a classic tragedy and a TV sitcom have no significant features in common, or that a slave narrative has no literary qualities that might make it worth teaching, or that politics and literature do not mix. This habit of questioning what seems like common sense is what makes theorists a nuisance, forcing us to give reasons for assumptions that we once could take for granted, as Socrates irritated his fellow Athenians by insisting that the unexamined life is not worth living.

The recent spread of theory as a sort of common currency across the cultural disciplines coincides with the erosion of consensus on the meaning of such central concepts as "literature," "literary value," "author," "reading," "politics," "tradition," "universality," and "culture," as these and many other concepts are thrown into the arena of theoretical discussion. Though this development stimulates arcane kinds of speculation, it only parallels what has been happening in society at large, as challenges to traditional sexual definitions, for example, force us into theoretical debates about the meanings of terms like "male" and "female." Theoretical controversy is not the monopoly of faddish literati. It is instanced in debates on abortion and gun control, occurs in lunchtime conversations, letters to the editor, and talk shows, and is everywhere else in the news.

In my sense of the term, then, OMP is as much a "theorist" as YFP, having been forced by her disagreement to articulate his traditional view of literature as a theory, something he would not have had to do a few decades ago. Though most contemporary theory is critical of traditional ideas of culture, there is nothing intrinsically antitraditional about theory. On the contrary, it is perfectly possible to defend the infusion of theory into the curriculum on traditional grounds—namely, that students have a right to understand the rationale underlying what they are being taught, to know why they should do what they are being asked to do. In this respect the real enemy of tradition is the kind of "traditional" teaching that is content to hand on received tastes and values without investigating the assumptions behind them.

Attacks on theory—like the one mounted by Robert Alter in his recent book *The Pleasures of Reading in an Ideological Age*[14]— are really attacks on the uncomfortable eruption of conflict into areas formerly governed by a certain gentleman's agreement. The complaint that literature is being driven out by theory, which is the burden of Alter's first chapter, entitled "The Disappearance of Reading," is really a complaint that interpretation has become overly controversial. In a favorable review of Alter's book, Denis Donoghue actually calls for a "trouble-free zone of reading" that would keep literature and its shell-shocked readers safe.[15] What looks to Alter like the disappearance of reading is a group of new ways of reading that he dislikes. There is, alas, no trouble-free zone of reading. The problem with attacking disagreement and conflict is that you only tend to provoke more disagreement and conflict—that is, more theoretical debate. Disagreement seems to be the one thing it is futile to disagree with.

Turning the Problem into the Solution

WHAT seems to me most unfortunate about the theoretical disagreement between OMP and YFP is not *that* it is taking place but *where* it is taking place, behind the educational scenes where their students cannot learn anything from it. For disagreements about "Dover Beach" are not peripheral to humanistic culture; they are central to what we mean by humanistic culture in a society where controversy is increasingly the rule rather than the exception.

This is not to say that all faculty debates are worth presenting to undergraduates or that debates on the politics of reading are the best place to begin an introduction to literature. I believe, however, that if OMP's apathetic students could witness the debate I have presented, they would be more likely to get excited about "Dover Beach" than they are now. They might also find it easier to make out the sense of the poem, for the controversy over it might give them the sort of context for reading it that they probably lack. It might even give them a reason to look up the whereabouts of Dover Beach.

Then again, it might not. The controversy would have to be presented in a way that avoids the pedantry, obscurity, and technicality to which academics are notoriously prone. And even when these vices are avoided, some students will have as much trouble seeing why they should interest themselves in a critical debate over "Dover Beach" as in "Dover Beach" itself. Student alienation from academic intellectual culture runs deep and may deepen further as the terms of that culture become ever more confusingly in dispute.

This, however, is all the more reason for teaching the debate. As students move from OMP's to YFP's course, and to many others beyond, the curriculum exposes them to a latent conversation of texts, ideas, and values. But since they experience that conversation only as a series of noncommunicating monologues, they understandably have trouble recognizing it *as* a conversation at all. Curricular disjunction has been a problem for students since the advent of specialized departments and the elective system a century ago, but students pay a steeper educational price for this problem today than in the past because there is less and less tacit common ground to fall back on. OMP and YFP are farther apart in their key assumptions than literature teachers used to be, farther apart even in what they assume about what can be legitimately controversial. If it goes without saying in YFP's class that literature is inevitably political and it goes without saying in OMP's class that such a view is preposterous, the results are likely to be profoundly confusing for the student who goes from one to the other. When premises that were once placidly taken for granted by authorities become disputed, it is difficult for students to be sure whose story to believe—or even to be sure what the range of conflicting stories is. And without a grasp of the conflicting stories, it is difficult to become competent at constructing your own story.

E. D. Hirsch has convinced many of us that college students know less today than they did in the past. If this is the case (and I raise some questions about the assumption in Chapter 5), one reason may be that there is a good deal more to know today than there was in the past. The more there is to know, the harder it is to be sure which part of it all you are supposed to remember. And it figures to be harder still if your teachers differ, in ways that you never see correlated, about what it is important to remember.

The remedy for this state of educational "fragmentation" has always been to seek a consensus that will somehow pull the fragments together in a synthesis. Such a consensus has rarely proved achievable in the past, and it seems even less likely to do so today. It is time to recognize that arriving at consensus is not the only way to pull a curriculum together, that difference can be a basis for coherence if it is openly engaged rather than kept out of sight.

Any course can be a place to start. When an article containing a version of the lounge debate appeared in *Harper's,* I passed out copies to an undergraduate literature class along with the text of "Dover Beach." True, the debate as I have staged it is reductive, but in teaching, one often has to *start out* with a reduction in order to go anywhere beyond. In my class, discussion followed a pattern similar to that of the debate itself: an initial polarization of interpretations, which became less stark as participants modified their positions, alternative positions emerged, and those who started out on one side moved to another. Some students took OMP's side, some YFP's, and some argued that neither position was adequate or that the issues needed to be reframed. This, in my experience, is the usual effect of teaching the conflicts: not that everyone becomes locked into entrenched positions (although that can happen) but that the terms of the polarization are themselves challenged and displaced by alternative ways of framing the issues. With less of a vested interest in one side or the other, students can often spot points of agreement that their teachers overlook. One student said that while he sided with OMP, struggling to refute YFP made "Dover Beach" clearer and more interesting to him than when he had read the poem in high school, where it had been assigned simply as a model of poetic greatness. Several said the debate helped illuminate disagreements that were coming up in other courses, including ones outside the humanities.

It became clear during my experiment that my students' interest in the discussion was greatly heightened by the public prominence of the debate outside the university. Students brought editorials to class that had appeared in that day's newspaper; there is nothing like being bashed in the morning paper for your kind's crimes against the humanities for stimulating a provocative discussion in your afternoon class. I began to realize that as misleading as it has frequently been, the media publicity about the culture war has already been educating students without the intervention of any curriculum committee. Having watched the debate on "Nightline," "Firing Line," or the "MacNeil / Lehrer Newshour," my students came into my course at least knowing that the humanities are not the scene of placid conviviality they have pretended to be. The publicity made academic concerns suddenly *real* to them as they had not seemed before, and it gave us a shared reference point that we would not have previously had.

I also noticed something else: Discovering that their teachers were at odds did not seem to make these students think less of us, as I might have expected. On the contrary, it was as if the sight of us becoming angry and agitated made us seem a bit more human, less the image of imperturbability that so often makes teachers seem remote and forbidding to students. Nor, once they adjusted to it, did these students seem as disoriented as some colleagues warned me they would become at being thrown into a situation in which they had to formulate answers for themselves from conflicting alternatives rather than have them handed to them. They had grown up in America, after all, where clashing authorities are not an unusual experience. I suspect we teachers sometimes use our students' supposed unpreparedness for controversy as an excuse to avoid it ourselves.

The idea of teaching the conflicts has been endorsed by a major educational association, several prominent educational officials, and two important figures identified with opposing sides in the culture war. Henry Louis Gates remarks that "there's nothing to be embarrassed about: college isn't kindergarten; our job isn't to present a seemingly dignified, unified front to the students."[16] Diane Ravitch, who elsewhere makes the standard neoconservative complaints about divisive tendencies in multiculturalism, speaks more constructively when she argues (with reference to the high school curriculum) that "where genuine controversies exist, they should be taught and debated in the classroom."

Ravitch writes as follows:

If scholars disagree, students should know it. One great advantage of this approach is that students will see that history is a lively study, that textbooks are fallible, that historians disagree, that the writing of history is influenced by the historians' politics and ideology, that history is written by people who make choices among alternative facts and interpretations, and that history changes as new facts are uncovered and new interpretations win adherents.

An example suggested by Ravitch of the kind of disputed question that could profitably be taken up in school history courses is, "Was Egypt a black civilization?" She asks: "Why not raise the question, read the arguments of the different sides in the debate, show slides of Egyptian pharaohs and queens, read books about life in ancient Egypt, invite guest scholars from the local university, and visit museums with Egyptian collections?"[17] Ravitch suggests that the discussion might include the broader debate provoked by various black scholars and by Martin Bernal in *Black Athena*, who argue that Egypt's profound influence on the culture of classical Greece was written out of history in the nineteenth century, when it conflicted with the emergent racist theory that black Africa had no civilization. Supplementary readings could include some of the many special issues or feature articles that national magazines such as *Time*, the *New Republic*, and *Newsweek* have devoted to the controversy ("Was Cleopatra Black?"). Even a teacher who rejects the Bernal Thesis can probably teach ancient history more meaningfully and effectively by making it a reference point.

As the Egyptian example shows, taking a contemporary controversy as one's starting point in no way restricts a course merely to contemporary concerns. The critic Lawrence Lipking has pointed out that the famous seventeenth-century Battle of the Books in England and France anticipated many of the issues that occupy us today, including "the canon debate, historical revisionism, the tension between theory and practice, and not least questions about the worth of civilization itself."[18] That past debates over the "canon" centered on scriptural texts rather than secular ones suggests how the current debate could be used to link literary and religious studies.

Courses of the kind I have described above are a start, but for reasons I have suggested, to make qualitative improvements in education, it will be necessary to move beyond the single insular course and begin integrating the curricular pieces. In Chapter 9 we will look at some existing programs that are finding ways to do so without adding to the faculty work load or the college budget (integration should actually *save* money by reducing wasteful duplication). These programs show we can actually do something to counteract the centrifugal tendencies of the curriculum instead of ritualistically bewailing fragmentation, and they provide a model for turning the poisonous divisions of the culture war into educationally valuable discussion.*

This seems to me a more promising way to achieve the "clear educational vision" that former Secretary of Education Bennett urges on us. Instead of reacting defensively to the challenge of multiculturalism, treating it only as a lamentable symptom of "the disuniting of America," we would start to heal wounds by respectfully engaging various multiculturalist arguments (often almost as much at odds with one another as with critics outside the movement) within the curriculum itself. Instead of endlessly attacking divisiveness, we would engage insurgents' arguments in an arena where students could learn from the debate, take part in it, and make their own informed choices. Instead of trying to ground the curriculum in a predefined common culture in which we all agree on Bennett's or someone else's approved list of books, thinkers, and ideas, we would ground it in a common discussion and see how much consensus emerges. The curriculum would then begin to look less like a cafeteria than a symposium in which for once we talk to one another rather than past one another.

Sparked by the current debate, numerous colleges and departments are now making a serious attempt to reform their general education courses and introductory courses for majors. This development is extremely encouraging. But despite hours spent in faculty meetings, such efforts too often founder: Either

---

*Teaching the conflicts has potential applicability to museums as well as classrooms. In an unpublished essay W. J. T. Mitchell has suggested that debates could profitably be used to organize the sort of museum collections on Egypt that Ravitch mentions. Mitchell proposes that when an exhibit deals with controversial materials, museums should incorporate the controversy into the exhibit itself. In the two major cases of 1990, the allegedly pornographic Robert Mapplethorpe photographs in Cincinnati and the "West as America" Smithsonian exhibit that challenged traditionally idealized representations of the American West, the angry reactions that ensued might have been more edifying had the controversies over pornographic art and historical revision been made part of the explicit concern of the exhibits themselves.

the college or department is unable to get agreement on the content of these courses, or—more often—in order to get that agreement, it accepts a bland compromise that results in no significant change. Such failures are inevitable as long as colleges and departments persist in thinking of their conflicts as something they somehow must get *over with* before they can plan a coherent introductory course or major. Unfortunately it tends not to occur to anyone that the differences of principle that are aired in the faculty meetings would make a more lively and instructive set of introductory courses than any of the options being debated.

My experience convinces me that the controversies from which we have been trying to protect "Dover Beach" can do a lot to save it. They can also do a lot to heal the Balkanization and isolationism that so many are complaining about. Francis Oakley, professor of history and president of Williams College, writes:

> [T]he great interpretative disputes that currently agitate and energize the humanities and social sciences are no more to be wished away today than were the truly subversive novelties of Aristotelian metaphysics in the thirteenth century. . . . Nor will we serve our students well if, in constructing our curricula, we attempt to sidle around contemporary disputes and dilemmas. For some of us, I believe, the great pedagogic challenge for the immediate future will be that of inserting those disputes, instead, into the heart of our teaching endeavor.[19]

Chapter 4

Hidden Meaning, or, Disliking Books at an Early Age

I LIKE to think I have a certain advantage as a teacher of literature because when I was growing up I disliked and feared books. My youthful aversion to books showed a fine impartiality, extending across the whole spectrum of literature, history, philosophy, science, and what by then (the late 1940s) had come to be called social studies. But had I been forced to choose, I would have singled out literature and history as the reading I disliked most. Science at least had some discernible practical use, and you could have fun solving the problems in the textbooks with their clear-cut answers. Literature and history had no apparent application to my experience, and any boy in my school who had cultivated them—I can't recall one who did—would have marked himself as a sissy.

As a middle-class Jew growing up in an ethnically mixed Chicago neighborhood, I was already in danger of being beaten up daily by rougher working-class boys. Becoming a bookworm would have only given them a decisive reason for beating me up. Reading and studying were more permissible for girls, but they, too, had to be careful not to get too intellectual, lest they acquire the stigma of being "stuck up."

In *Lives on the Boundary,* a remarkable autobiography of the making of an English teacher, Mike Rose describes how the "pain and confusion" of his working-class youth made "school and knowledge" seem a saving alternative. Rose writes of feeling "freed, as if I were untying fetters," by his encounters with certain college teachers, who helped him recognize that "an engagement with ideas could foster competence and lead me out into the world."[1] Coming at things from my middle-class perspective, however, I took for granted a freedom that school, knowledge, and engagement with ideas seemed only to threaten.

My father, a literate man, was frustrated by my refusal to read anything besides comic books, sports magazines, and the John R. Tunis and Clair Bee sports novels. I recall his once confining me to my room until I finished a book on the voyages of Magellan, but try as I might, I could do no better than stare bleakly at the pages. I could not, as we would later say, "relate to" Magellan or to any of the other books my father brought home—detective stories, tales of war and heroism, adventure stories with adolescent heroes (the *Hardy Boys, Hans Brinker, or The Silver Skates*), stories of scientific discovery (Paul de Kruif's *Microbe Hunters*), books on current events. Nothing worked.

It was understood, however, that boys of my background would go to college and that once there we would get serious and buckle down. For some, "getting serious" meant prelaw, premed, or a major in business to prepare for taking over the family business. My family did not own a business, and law and medicine did not interest me, so I drifted by default into the nebulous but conveniently noncommittal territory of the liberal arts. I majored in English.

At this point the fear of being beaten up if I were caught having anything to do with books was replaced by the fear of flunking out of college if I did not learn to deal with them. But though I dutifully did my homework and made good grades (first at the University of Illinois, Chicago branch, then at the University of Chicago, from which I graduated in 1959), I continued to find "serious" reading painfully difficult and alien. My most vivid recollections of college reading are of assigned classics I failed to finish: *The Iliad* (in the Richmond Lattimore translation); *The Autobiography of Benvenuto Cellini,* a major disappointment after the paperback jacket's promise of "a lusty classic of Renaissance ribaldry"; E. M. Forster's *Passage to India,* sixty agonizing pages of which I managed to slog through before giving up. Even Hemingway, Steinbeck, and Fitzgerald, whose contemporary world was said to be "close to my own experience," left me cold. I saw little there that did resemble my experience.

Even when I had done the assigned reading, I was often tongue-tied and embarrassed when called on. What was unclear to me was what I was supposed to *say* about literary works, and why. Had I been born a decade or two earlier, I might have come to college with the rudiments of a literate vocabulary for talking about culture that some people older than I acquired through family, high school, or church. As it was, "cultured" phrases seemed effete and sterile to me. When I was able to produce the kind of talk that was required in class, the intellectualism of it came out sounding stilted and hollow in my mouth. If *Cliffs Notes* and other such crib sheets for the distressed had yet come into existence, with their ready-to-copy summaries of widely taught literary works, I would have been an excellent customer. (As it was, I did avail myself of the primitive version then in existence called *Masterplots.*)

What first made literature, history, and other intellectual pursuits seem attractive to me was exposure to critical debates. There was no single conversion experience, but a gradual transformation over several years, extending into my first teaching positions, at the University of New Mexico and then Northwestern University. But one of the first sparks I remember was a controversy over *The Adventures of Huckleberry Finn* that arose in a course during my junior year in college. On first attempt, Twain's novel was just another assigned classic that I was too bored to finish. I could see little connection between my Chicago upbringing and Huck's pre-Civil War adventures with a runaway slave on a raft up the Mississippi.

My interest was aroused, however, when our instructor mentioned that the critics had disagreed over the merits of the last part of the novel. He quoted Ernest Hemingway's remark that "if you read [the novel] you must stop where the nigger Jim is stolen by the boys. This is the real end. The rest is cheating." According to this school of thought, the remainder of the book trivializes the quest for Jim's freedom that has motivated the story up to that point. This happens first when Jim becomes an object of Tom Sawyer's slapstick humor, then when it is revealed that unbeknownst to Huck, the reader, and himself, Jim has already been freed by his benevolent owner, so that the risk we have assumed Jim and Huck to be under all along has been really no risk at all.

Like the critics, our class divided over the question: Did Twain's ending vitiate the book's profound critique of racism, as Hemingway's charge of cheating implied? Cheating in my experience up to then was something students did, an unthinkable act for a famous author. It was a revelation to me that famous authors were capable not only of mistakes but of ones that even lowly undergraduates might be able to point out. When I chose to write my term paper on the dispute over the ending, my instructor suggested I look at several critics on the opposing sides, T. S. Eliot and Lionel Trilling, who defended the ending, and Leo Marx, who sided with Hemingway.

Reading the critics was like picking up where the class discussion had left off, and I gained confidence from recognizing that my classmates and I had had thoughts that, however stumbling our expression of them, were not too far from the thoughts of famous published critics. I went back to the novel again and to my surprise found myself rereading it with an excitement I had never felt before with a serious book. Having the controversy over the ending in mind, I now had some issues *to watch out for* as I read, issues that reshaped the way I read the earlier chapters as well as the later ones and focused my attention. And having issues to watch out for made it possible not only to concentrate, as I had not been able to do earlier, but to put myself in the text—to read with a sense of personal engagement that I had not felt before. Reading the novel with the voices of the critics running through my mind, I found myself thinking of things that I might say about what I was reading, things that may have belonged partly to the critics but also now belonged to me. It was as if having a stock of things to look for and to say about a literary work had somehow made it possible for me to read one.

One of the critics had argued that what was at issue in the debate over *Huckleberry Finn* was not just the novel's value but its cultural significance: If *Huckleberry Finn* was contradictory or confused in its attitude toward race, then what did that say about the culture that had received the novel as one of its representative cultural documents and had made Twain a folk hero? This critic had also made the intriguing observation—I found out only later it was a critical commonplace at that time—that judgments about the novel's aesthetic value could not be separated from judgments about its moral substance. I recall taking in both this critic's arguments and the cadence of the phrases in which they were couched; perhaps it would not be so bad after all to become the sort of person who talked about "cultural contradictions" and the "inseparability of form and content." Perhaps even mere literary-critical talk could give you a certain power in the real world. As the possibility dawned on me that reading and intellectual discussion might actually have something to do with my real life, I became less embarrassed about using the intellectual formulas.

The Standard Story

IT was through exposure to such critical reading and discussion over a period of time that I came to catch the literary bug, eventually choosing the vocation of teaching. This was not the way it is supposed to happen. In the standard story of academic vocation that we like to tell ourselves, the germ is first planted by an early experience of literature itself. The future teacher is initially inspired by some primary experience of a great book and only subsequently acquires the secondary, derivative skills of critical discussion. A teacher may be involved in instilling this inspiration, but a teacher who seemingly effaces himself or herself before the text. Any premature or excessive acquaintance with secondary critical discourse, and certainly with its sectarian debates, is thought to be a corrupting danger, causing one to lose touch with the primary passion for literature.

This, as we have seen, is the charge leveled against the current generation of literature teachers, who are said to have become so obsessed with sophisticated critical theories that they have lost the passion they once had for literature itself. They have been seduced by professionalism, drawn away from a healthy absorption in literature to the sickly fascination with analysis and theory and to the selfish advancement of their careers. This hostility to recent theory would not be so powerful, however, if it were not overlaid on a set of older resentments which long predate the rise of deconstruction and poststructuralism, resentments at literature's having become an academic "field" to begin with. Today's attacks on literary theory are often really attacks on literary criticism, or at least on criticism of the intensely analytic kind that academics practice, which has always been suspected of coming between readers (and students) and the primary experience of literature itself. This resentment is rooted in anxieties about the increasing self-consciousness of modern life, which often leaves us feeling that we are never quite living but only endlessly talking about it, too often in some abstract professional vocabulary. The anxieties are expressed in our romantic literary tradition, which protests against urban forms of sophistication that, it is believed, cause us to lose touch with the innocence of childhood and with our creative impulses.

To those who have never reconciled themselves to the academicization of literature, the seeming overdevelopment of academic criticism with its obtrusive methodology and its endless disputes among interpretations and theories seems a betrayal not just of literature and the common reader but of the professor's own original passion for literature. In a recent letter to an intellectual journal one writer suggests that we should be concerned less about the often-lamented common reader whom academic critics have deserted than about "the souls of the academics and literati themselves, who, as a result of social and professional pressures, have lost touch with the inner impulses that drew them to the world of books in the first place."[2] What this writer cannot imagine is that someone might enter academic literary study because he actually *likes* thinking and talking in an analytical or theoretical way about books and that such a person might see his acceptance of "professional pressures" not as a betrayal of the "inner impulses" that drew him "to the world of books in the first place" but as a way to fulfill those impulses.

The standard story ascribes innocence to the primary experience of literature and sees the secondary experience of professional criticism as corrupting. In my case, however, things had evidently worked the other way around: I had to be corrupted first in order to experience innocence. It was only when I was introduced to a critical debate about *Huckleberry Finn* that my helplessness in the face of the novel abated and I could experience a personal reaction to it. Getting into immediate contact with the text was for me a curiously triangular business; I could not do it directly but needed a conversation of other readers to give me the issues and terms that made it possible to respond.

As I think back on it now, it was as if the critical conversation I needed had up to then been withheld from me, on the ground that it could only interfere with my direct access to literature itself. The assumption was that leaving me alone with literary texts themselves, uncontaminated by the interpretations and theories of professional critics, would enable me to get on the closest possible terms with those texts. But being alone with the texts only left me feeling bored and helpless, since I had no language with which to make them mine. On the one hand, I was being asked to speak a foreign language—literary criticism—while on the other hand, I was being protected from that language, presumably for my own safety.

The moral I draw from this experience is that our ability to read well depends more than we think on our ability to *talk* well about what we read. Our assumptions about what is "primary" and "secondary" in the reading process blind us to what actually goes on. Many literate people learned certain ways of talking about books so long ago that they have forgotten they ever had to learn them. These people therefore fail to understand the reading problems of the struggling students who have still not acquired a critical vocabulary.

How typical my case was is hard to say, but many of the students I teach seem to have grown up as the same sort of nonintellectual, nonbookish person I was, and they seem to view literature with some of the same aversions, fears, and anxieties. That is why I like to think it is an advantage for a teacher to know what it feels like to grow up being indifferent to literature and intimidated by criticism and what it feels like to overcome a resistance to talking like an intellectual.

Just Read the Books

THE standard story of how we learn to read provides little help in dealing with such problems. Seeing criticism (and critical

debate) as a distraction from the "primary" experience of literature itself, the standard story implies that the business of teaching literature is basically simple: Just put the student in front of
a good book, provide teachers who are encouraging and helpful,
and the rest presumably will take care of itself. The traditional
maxim that sums up this view is that a good book "essentially
teaches itself." The great teacher is one who knows how to let
the book teach itself. And it is true that in the spell cast by such
a teacher, it often *seems* as if the work itself is speaking directly
to the student without intervention from the teacher's interpretations and theories. But this spell is an illusion. If books really
taught themselves, there would be no reason to attend classes;
students could simply stay home and read them on their own.

Nevertheless, the standard story remains seductive. Much of
the appeal of Allan Bloom's *The Closing of the American Mind* lies
in its eloquent restatement of the standard story, with its reas-
suringly simple view of reading and teaching: ". . . a liberal education means reading certain generally recognized classic texts,
just reading them, letting them dictate what the questions are
and the method of approaching them—not forcing them into
categories we make up, not treating them as historical products,
but trying to read them as their authors wished them to be read."[3]
What has gone wrong, Bloom suggests, is that instead of letting
the texts themselves dictate the questions we ask about them, a
generation of overly professionalized teachers has elevated its
own narcissistic interests over those of the author and the students. These teachers, as Bloom puts it, engage in "endless debates
about methods—among Freudian criticism, Marxist criticism,
New Criticism, Structuralism and Deconstructionism, and many
others, all of which have in common the premise that what Plato
or Dante had to say about reality is unimportant."[4]

It sounds so commonsensical that only a desiccated academic
could disagree. What could be more obvious than the difference
between "just" reading books, as ordinary readers have always
done, and imposing theories, methodologies, and isms on books,

as methodology-crazed academics do? The question, however, is whether anyone ever "just" reads a book in the way Bloom describes. We need go no further than Bloom's own quoted statements to see that he himself does not practice the doctrine he preaches. When Bloom invokes the names of Plato and Dante, he does *not* let these authors dictate the questions that govern his discussion but "forces" them into categories he, Allan Bloom, with his twentieth-century preoccupations, has "made up." After all, what did Plato and Dante know about Freudians, Marxists, cultural relativists, and the other contemporary targets of Bloom's polemic? In using Plato and Dante to attack the intellectual and educational trends of his own time, Bloom is not reading these writers as they wished to be read but is *applying* them to a set of contexts they did not and could not have anticipated. This is not to say that Bloom is unfaithful to Plato's text, only that he does not passively take dictation from Plato's text but actively selects from it for his own purposes—just as he accuses theorists of doing.

Richard Rorty has succinctly pointed out the trouble with Bloom's "just read the books" theory. Rorty acknowledges that interpreters are obliged "to give authors a run for their money," respecting "an author's way of talking and thinking, trying to put ourselves in her shoes." He argues, however, that "it is not clear how we can avoid forcing books into 'categories we make up. . . .' " We cannot help reading books, Rorty says, "with questions in mind—not questions dictated by the books, but questions we have previously, if vaguely formulated."[5] Rorty's point is not that reading is merely subjective but that it is inevitably *selective*. It is not that any reading of Plato is as good as any other but that even the most reliable reading has to select certain aspects of the text to emphasize, and the selection will be conditioned by the contingent situations in which the text is read.

I would restate Rorty's point this way: As readers we are necessarily concerned with *both* the questions posed by the text and the questions we bring to the text from our own differing interests and cultural backgrounds. Bloom thinks he can choose between "just reading" Plato and Dante and applying a "method" to them as do academic Freudians and Marxists. But Bloom's way of reading, which is influenced by his mentor the philosopher Leo Strauss, is as much a "method" as any other, bringing its special set of interests and principles of selection that are not dictated by Plato and Dante.

If the "just read the books" theory is dubious as a general account of reading, it is disastrous when it guides the teaching of literature, where texts are not simply read but made the objects of sophisticated conversations in which students are expected to participate. What the theory obscures is that no matter how humble and self-effacing teachers may try to be, they inevitably teach *themselves* in the process of teaching Plato, Dante, or any other text or subject. In order to teach Plato's *Republic,* one must consider—if only unconsciously—not just how Plato may have wished to be read but such questions as which aspects of Plato does it now seem most necessary to agree or quarrel with. Which aspects are likely to be understandable without explanation to anyone living today, and which are likely to seem obscure, perverse, or even unintelligible to a modern audience—as Plato's absolutist view of truth or his hierarchical view of society may be in a postscientific, postdemocratic age? And once a second author is introduced into the course—Dante, say, or Shakespeare—"just" reading or teaching Plato as he presumably would have wished to be read and taught is even more out of the question since one is now teaching a relation between Plato and a writer he knew nothing about.

In teaching any text, one necessarily teaches an interpretation of it. This seems so obvious as to be hardly worth restating, but what follows from it is not obvious and is resisted violently by many who oppose the spread of theory. It follows that what literature teachers teach is not literature but criticism, or literature as it is filtered through a grid of analysis, interpretation, and theory. "Remarks are not literature," said Gertrude Stein in a now-celebrated observation, and Stein was right: Teachers cannot avoid interposing "remarks" between literature and their students—remarks, we hope, that illuminate the works and help our students take personal possession of them, but remarks nevertheless.

If teachers cannot avoid translating the literature they teach into some critical language or other, neither can students, for criticism, as I suggested above, is the language students are expected to speak and are punished for not speaking well. Inevitably the students who do well in school and college are those who learn to talk more or less like their teachers, who learn to produce something resembling Intellectualspeak, as we might call it. Nobody is born knowing how to talk and write Intellectualspeak. By what process do we imagine students will acquire this language? The assumption seems to be that it will happen by a kind of osmosis, as students internalize the talk that goes on in class until they are able to produce a reasonable facsimile of it. However, as a recent textbook writer, Gordon Harvey, points out, not all students "can make this translation, since it requires that they intuit a whole set of intellectual moves and skills . . . too basic for experienced writers even to notice themselves carrying out."[6] The polite fiction that students will learn to make these "intellectual moves" by being in the presence of them for several hours a week is usually just that, a polite fiction.

Again, the problem is that what students are able to say about a text depends not just on the text but on their relation to a critical community of readers, a "discourse community" which over time has developed an agenda of problems, issues, and questions with respect both to specific authors and texts and to culture generally. (This point has been forcefully developed by discourse community theorists like Patricia Bizzell.)[7] When students are screened from this critical community and its debates, or when they experience only the fragmentary and disconnected versions of it represented by a series of courses, they are likely either to be tongue-tied in the face of the text itself or to respond in a limited personal idiom, like the student who "relates to" Hamlet because he, too, had a mean stepfather.

In a paradoxical way, then, the more we try to protect the teaching of literature itself from the "interference" of criticism and theory, the more customers we produce for *Cliffs Notes*. It is easy to deplore *Cliffs Notes* as a prostitution of learning without recognizing how dependent students become on such crutches when we fail to think through the problem of socializing them into the academic intellectual community. It is also easy to blind ourselves to the pedagogical lessons that *Cliffs Notes* might teach us. Since their livelihood depends on it, the creators of *Cliffs Notes* have a more immediate incentive than educators do to determine what it is that students are actually supposed to do in literature courses, as opposed to whatever is officially believed or claimed. The producers of *Cliffs Notes* know what educators often ignore, which is that most students need special help to produce a kind of literary-critical talk that is rarely spoken outside the literature class or the book review pages.

The literary theorist Gregory Jay sums up the point well:

> We tend to forget the fact that reading is an unnatural act—left alone, no child would do it. Reading must be taught, which means that the child's discovery of books never takes place in an edenic state of nature, but in a cultural setting that is steeped in assumptions, information, prejudices, and other cultural baggage. The child is taught not only to sound out the words, but to interpret their meaning—which is to say that literary criticism is there from the moment the child's parents begin to read to him or her or explain the meanings of signs on the street.[8]

It is easy to forget the "cultural baggage" that infused literary criticism into our reading processes from the start and to believe that our literary receptivity sprang spontaneously from an encounter with literary texts in themselves. From this it seems to follow that if a student fails, as I did, to show such receptivity, it is because he is not being exposed to enough literature, or enough of the right kind of literature, or because professional criticism is getting in the way.

In short, reading books with comprehension, making arguments, writing papers, and making comments in a class discussion are *social* activities. They involve entering into a cultural or disciplinary conversation, a process not unlike an initiation into a social club. We obscure this social dimension when we conceive of education as if it were a process of contemplating important truths, values, and "cultural literacy" information in a vacuum and consequently treat such student tasks as reading assignments, making arguments, writing papers, and entering class discussions as if they were a matter of performing certain abstract procedures in a social void. Choose a topic that interests you, freshman writers are told; organize your paper logically around a central idea, and remember to support your thesis with specific illustration and evidence. Such advice is usually more paralyzing than helpful because it factors out the social conversation that reading, writing, and arguing must be part of in order to become personally meaningful.

Choosing a topic that interests you or making an effective argument depends on having a sense of what *other people* are saying, of what the state of the discussion is. Before my exposure to the critical debate on *Huckleberry Finn,* I had been trying to generate that discussion out of myself, something I did not know how to do. Exposure to the debate made me less of an outsider, provided me with a social community that gave my reading a stimulus and direction. I could now discover what my teachers meant by "enjoying literature" because this had ceased to be a matter of vainly struggling to achieve some mysterious and rarefied experience. Relation to a community made the intimacy of literary experience possible.

Of course, I was lucky in some ways, lucky that the critical articles I was given were ones that at that stage I could handle. Mere exposure to literary criticism is no panacea. Recalling his college days in *Lives on the Boundary,* Mike Rose describes his problems trying to read a collection of essays on art and culture by the critic Jacques Barzun:

> I remember starting one essay and stopping, adrift, two pages later. Then another, but no go. The words arose from a depth of knowledge and a developed perception and a wealth of received ways to talk about art and a seemingly endless reserve of allusions. I felt like a janitor at a gallery opening, silent, intimidated, little flecks of knowledge—Bagehot, Stendhal, baroque ideology—sticking to the fiber of my broom.[9]

By what process do some students eventually outgrow such feelings and become fluent intellectuals like Rose, whereas others with the same will to do so do not? How the intellectual community presents itself to them has a lot to do with it, I think, and that, as we shall see, is influenced by the way the curriculum is organized.

Dueling Jargons

STUDYING literature is never a matter of "just" reading great texts but always involves a choice of critical vocabularies and theories. But which vocabularies and theories? Today's battle lines are drawn not only between competing kinds of texts but between the critical vocabularies in which the texts are taught. On the one hand, we have the traditional vocabulary of criticism, seemingly clear, humane, responsible to the reader and the text. On the other, we evidently have a proliferation of perverse jargons, many of which seem to be aimed at excluding the common reader and asserting the superiority of the critic or theorist to the creative artist.

What possible excuse is there for the apparently barbarous, ideologically loaded jargon in which so much academic criticism has come to be written? One excuse is the need for a shorthand. If I can say, "We need to problematize that distinction," it saves me the trouble of having to use a wordy formulation such as "We need to show why that distinction is not as self-evident and uncontroversial as its users think." Often underlying such jargon, however, is a kind of alienation device like those employed by the playwright Bertolt Brecht—a deliberate attempt to alienate readers from their normal expectations. Unfortunately the effect too often is simply to alienate readers without changing their thinking. Nevertheless, to speak of a literary work as an "inscription of signifying practices" instead of as an expression of the "creative imagination" is a way of suggesting that literature is a social product, enmeshed in a system of more mundane cultural assumptions, texts, and "discourses," not an autonomous creation springing full-blown from the brain of an unconditioned genius. The jargon is a way of shifting attention to the "cultural work" done by the text, suggesting that the text does not stand above its culture but acts on and is acted on by it. It points to the conflicts, contradictions, and struggles in works of literature rather than the unifying elements.

The more deeply embroiled we become in this clash of philosophies and vocabularies, the more important it will seem which vocabulary wins. Yet as fundamental as the differences between the old and new vocabularies may be, they are minor when compared with the difference that separates both of them from the vocabulary of those who do not speak literary criticism at all and thus find both old and new versions of the dialect equally strange. As much as traditional humanists and theorists may dislike each other, to a person who is not sure what the words "humanist" and "theorist" mean, these antagonists will look like two peas in a pod. In fact, the point can virtually be elevated into a general law: To noneggheads, any two eggheads, however antagonistic ideologically, will seem far similar to each other than to people like themselves.

To such laypeople, even the slogans of so-called traditional literary study—"humanistic values," "Western cultural tradition," "determinate meaning," "tragic vision," and so forth—are likely to sound as jargon-ridden and academic as talk about "signifying practices." To them, both the old and the new critical idioms represent a kind of insider trading in a market in which they have nothing invested. (For that matter, "insider trading" in its financial sense was incomprehensible jargon until recent scandals made it a household term.)

Critics who inveigh against the barbarity of today's theoretical jargon apply a double standard: They never ask how the supposedly less alienating language of traditional criticism may look to people not at home with it. Robert Alter, for example, in *The Pleasures of Reading in an Ideological Age,* adduces the following unidentified example of the bad writing perpetrated by today's "new literary technocrats": "Everywhere there are moving barriers and a-signifying elements which point to desiring production outside the oedipal domain and rend apart repressive totalities, a testament to Kafka's experimental machine." Alter comments: "It goes without saying that the proverbial common reader would be able to make little of this." No doubt this is true, and the example Alter chooses is grotesque enough. But after quoting it, Alter adds that the point it tries to make about Kafka "has been often stated not only more elegantly but also more instructively by critics who do not use this jargon. . . ." Here is Alter restating the point "more elegantly" and "instructively": "Kafka invents a mode of enigmatic fiction which taps an inchoate realm of the unconscious and defies conventional habits of interpretation."[10] Are common readers really likely to make much more of Alter's supposedly more lucid rewriting than they are of the original passage? When I presented the two passages to a class of undergraduates and asked them which was clearer, Alter's version came off only marginally better than the original. I would not be surprised if it were cited as yet another example of today's unintelligible jargon.

My point is not to excuse inappropriate jargon but to suggest that what you see as jargon is relative to the circles you are accustomed to moving in. Even the most clearly written criticism will be gibberish to people who have not been socialized into the literary or intellectual community. For these people, the problem is literary criticism *as such,* irrespective of its school or factional brand name, and the unintelligibility of criticism to them has less to do with its jargon than with the unfamiliarity of the issues with which it deals. Nobody would accuse the critic Jacques Barzun of academic obscurantism, yet I referred a moment ago to how opaque Barzun's criticism was to the young Mike Rose. Similarly, Alter's reference to "conventional habits of interpretation" will induce glassy stares in anyone not used to reflecting self-consciously on interpretive practices, whether the reference appears in *Critical Inquiry* or *The New York Times Book Review*.

This is not to say that recent theory is always as accessible as it should be—which is far from the truth—but that much of the inaccessibility for which current literary theorists are blamed is really a general feature of intellectual discourse. Moralistic attacks on jargon only obscure the issue.

Hidden Meaning

TO those not at home in the community of literary criticism, even supposedly plain words like "criticism" and "literature" sound like jargon. In fact, these words once sounded that way even inside that community: Some purists in the eighteenth century thought the word "criticize" unseemly, and the word "literature" denoted a gentleman's accomplishment not a special kind of imaginative writing. Today's barbaric jargon has a way of becoming tomorrow's standard usage (as the fate of psychoanalytic terms like "paranoid" illustrates), and the rate at which jargon is naturalized and domesticated varies unevenly from group to group. (Is "naturalize" jargon? It depends on who is reading this.) To the many for whom the word "criticism" still refers only to negative or sarcastic judgments, the nonpejorative use of "criticism" to mean analysis or explanation will be confusing.

When uninitiated students want to say what professional critics mean by "criticism," they say "book reports." For "literature," they may say "stories," denoting lyric poems, plays, novels, and essays, as in "I found Ralph Waldo Emerson's story 'Self-Reliance' very interesting." To a sophomore who thinks of literary texts as "stories" and of "criticism" as sarcastic remarks, talk of "traditional moral themes" will be not much less intimidating than "hegemonic discursive practices."

In the sophomore lexicon, in fact, the formula of choice is neither "themes" *nor* "discursive practices," but "hidden meaning," often coming in a nervously stammered question like "Professor X, do we always have to look for hidden meaning in these books?" Behind the question is often an inability to see why simple enjoyment of a literary work is not considered sufficient in the academy, why a student essay that accurately summarizes the plot of *Moby-Dick* but fails to discuss the symbolic meanings of the plot will earn a C. The academy's insistence on treating every literary work as a problem can easily seem perverse: What kind of person tries to *create* problems when they are not obvious already? The academic quest for "hidden meaning" implies that every text is a concealed set of problems and that if you don't see them, the problem is with you.

The students' lay usage derives from a perfectly sound insight, that the quest for "hidden meaning" (or "symbolism") is what classes in literature are largely all about. In fact, the quest for hidden meaning is what classes in most of the academic disciplines are about. What literary theorists call "thematizing" or "allegorization," ascribing abstract meanings to texts, events, and other phenomena that are not apparent to common sense, is the fundamental operation of intellectual culture, cutting across the divisions between the humanities, the social sciences, and perhaps even the physical sciences. The history professor who sees the sixteenth-century enclosure movement as a foreshadowing of capitalism, the economist who interprets a fluctuation of the market as a sign of impending recession, and the psychologist who analyzes a case study as a classic example of neurotic behavior are engaged in the same kind of thematizing activity as the English professor who teaches *Gulliver's Travels* as a profound statement about the human condition. For this reason, the demands of psychology, history, and literature courses may not seem so dissimilar to the struggling student, for they all involve the same daunting thematizing operations. In the dark all themes are gray.

This is not to say that there is anything specifically academic about these thematizing processes. We all use them every time we discuss whether a politician's speech means a tax increase is coming or whether the clouds on the horizon mean rain. But students who are not used to the academic forms of thematizing, who do not possess their special codes, have trouble recognizing that these forms are not fundamentally different from the kinds of generalizing and abstracting that they perform every day.

If hidden meaning is a problem in almost all academic subjects, however, it tends to be a special problem in literature courses, where the meanings ascribed to texts seem often to be drawn out of the instructor's hat like so many rabbits. Every literature teacher knows deep down that his students suspect— not necessarily without admiration—that what he does is "read into" texts meanings that are not really there. The process still seems vaguely like a trick even when the student learns to go through the motions well enough to get a good grade. I noted a moment ago that recent theorists like to argue that textual meaning is not natural but cultural, but for many students, textual meaning seems neither natural *nor* cultural but *magical*.

Humanists themselves are often ambivalent about their own obsessive preoccupation with hidden meanings, which smacks uncomfortably of a didactic approach that reduces works of art to a simplistic "moral" or "message." Sophisticated modern aesthetics is full of admonitions that in the words of Samuel Goldwyn, if it's a message you want, call Western Union. This attitude has been reinforced by pedagogical experience—namely, the perception that American students are already prone to a "message-hunting" approach to literature in which aesthetic factors are ignored, something not surprising in a culture where poetry has often meant Longfellow's "A Psalm of Life" ("Tell me not, in mournful numbers / Life is but an empty dream! . . .") or a homily by Edgar A. Guest ("It takes a heap o' livin' in a house t' make it home") embroidered and framed in the family parlor. Much of the literature teaching of the last two generations has been aimed at disabusing students of the belief that the message of *Macbeth* is adequately encapsulated in the statement that life is "a tale / Told by an idiot, full of sound and fury, / Signifying nothing." The New Critic Cleanth Brooks recalls that when he began teaching at Vanderbilt University in the 1930s, his students "actually approached Keats's 'Ode to a Nightingale' in the same spirit and with the same expectations with which they approached an editorial in the local country newspaper or an advertisement in the current Sears, Roebuck catalogue."[11]

Dissatisfaction with the message-hunting approach to literature has been reasonable enough. Yet it became somewhat misplaced when students like me started showing up, coming from homes in which "A Psalm of Life" was not displayed in the family parlor. My generation of college students, I think, did not generally acquire the conventional preconception which critics like Brooks aimed to disabuse us of: that literature exists to express uplifting messages. My main preconception was not that literature was uplifting but that it was boring, irrelevant, and mysterious. It was superfluous to warn me of the dangers of a message-hunting reading of *A Passage to India* when a message was just what I was struggling unsuccessfully to get from that novel.

Instead of trying to root out and extinguish the message-hunting approach to the arts, we teachers would be more straightforward if we acknowledged the inevitability of message hunting and thought more about how to help students formulate messages less reductively. Insofar as criticism is inevitably a sort of higher message hunting, students have to engage in it, and warning them against the practice can only be confusing. A teacher equipped with the latest high-powered decoding equipment who discourages students from message hunting is rather like a millionaire exhorting the poor not to be too concerned about material wealth. It is another instance of what I have described in this chapter, how our ambivalence about criticism and theory causes us to withhold from students the very languages that we expect them to produce.

Some, of course, will say that the hidden meanings we academics cherish are not "wealth" at all but the fool's gold that has corrupted literary education. The ability to formulate such meanings, however, to command the discourse about what texts and other social phenomena mean, to control what has come to be called "spin"—these are important forms of symbolic capital in a society where information is increasingly a key source of power. It seems time to come to terms with this fact, something which means seeing that education inevitably means socialization into the discussions and debates of an intellectual community. If we recognize that the control of spin can be an important issue in a presidential election, we should also be able to recognize that it is an issue in reading and teaching literature, that the words of Plato, Jane Austen, Ralph Ellison, and a TV soap are dependent on interpretation and theory, and that the meaning of any text is determined within a conversation of readers. If students are to learn to read and write better, then instead of shielding them from that conversation, we have to start making it more available to them.

Chapter 5

"Life of the Mind Stuff"

I N THE previous chapter I shifted the focus from our quarrels over competing texts and ideas to the difficulty all texts and ideas pose for the struggling student. Once that shift is made I think, it becomes clear that many of the defenses of high literacy to which we have lately been treated come from writers who either never experienced the predicament of such struggling students or else forgot what it was like once they had overcome it. In any case, the experience is hardly new or peculiar to the students of our own day, and I would like this chapter to be a reminder that there is more continuity than we have been led to think between the problems of today's students and those of yesterday. I also want to suggest how our attempts to diagnose these problems continue to suffer from certain long-standing confusions about the nature of intellectual *difficulty*, confusions about what makes a text or subject hard.

In his autobiography, *North Toward Home*, editor and writer Willie Morris offers a recollection of the fifties that rings truer to me than the nostalgic accounts we have received from writers like Cynthia Ozick. Morris says he is struck in reading the reminiscences of northern urban intellectuals by the vast difference between their adolescence and that of southerners like him. He mentions the autobiography of Alfred Kazin, who depicts his Brooklyn upbringing in the thirties as a struggle "for one set of ideas over others, for a fierce acceptance or rejection of one man's theories or another man's poetry." What a different kind of intellectual awakening, says Morris, was in store for those who went to college in the fifties "from places like Karnes City or Big Spring or Abilene or Rockdale or Yazoo City":

> [It] did not imply the victory of one set of ideologies over another, one way of viewing literature or politics over another, but something more basic and simple. This was the acceptance of ideas themselves as something worth living by. It was a matter, at the age of eighteen or nineteen, not of discovering *certain* books, but the simple *presence* of books. . . . [W]e at eighteen or nineteen were only barely beginning to learn that there *were* ideas. . . .[1]

Morris's point is easy to forget in the heat of today's culture war, when the need to line up with one set of books and ideas over another obscures the fact that the problem for most students has always been the "more basic and simple" one of learning to deal with books and ideas themselves.

The Age of the Gentleman's C

A LOOK at the social history of the American campus over the last century reminds us that the level of intellectual engagement in the American student body has never been inspiring. It is only relatively recently that more than a small minority of college students have taken the intellectual challenges of their courses seriously and have not been socially ostracized for doing so by their classmates.

This fact needs to be kept in mind when we assess today's

widespread alarms about declining literacy—not in order to minimize the seriousness of the problem but to keep it in perspective. In the measuring of today's educational failures, it is easy to succumb to a certain fantasy about the past in which undergraduates supposedly thrilled to the great books as expounded by inspirational and benevolent professors. We tend to remember our own education in an idealized way, forgetting the times we slept through the droning of the inspirational professors' courses or failed to finish the assignment. Anyone who thinks honestly about his or her high school experience will recall the ritual humiliation of "nerds" and "geeks" in glasses who read books.

If we take a long view going back to the turn of the century, there is reason to think that standards in higher education have actually *risen* rather than declined. It is well known that the past from which we are supposed to have declined was dominated by the infamous "gentleman's C" and by the ostracism from campus life of students who took intellectual work seriously. Conservatives who accuse affirmative action programs of lowering academic standards never mention the notorious standard for ignorance that was set by white male college students before women and minorities were permitted in large numbers on campus. It has been the steady pressure for reform from below that has raised academic standards by challenging the laziness and anti-intellectualism of the privileged classes.

To judge from the picture presented by Helen Lefkowitz Horowitz's excellent recent study *Campus Life,* it appears that in the formative period of the modern university immediately before and after World War I, professors rarely even *expected* that the majority of their students would actually read the assigned texts. Readers who have been persuaded by books like E. D. Hirsch's *Cultural Literacy* that the level of information possessed by college students has precipitously declined would do well to consider a statement made in 1911 by the president of the Modern

Language Association addressing his colleagues at the annual convention:

> You are all aware of how dangerous it is to assume, on the part of our college classes, any definite knowledge of any subject. Last year I had occasion to question a good many students about . . . Charlemagne; and one after another unblushingly assigned him to the eighteenth century. A colleague . . . could find no one in his class who knew what event is celebrated on the fourth of July. In a course in French literature, taken mainly by Juniors, a request to compare a certain drama with *Othello* drew forth the admission that a considerable part of the class knew nothing of Shakespeare's play. . . . You must have noticed how very difficult it has become for college students not only to write but to read their mother tongue. . . . The text has conveyed nothing to them, because they do not know the meaning of common English words.[2]

Were the students in 1911 who placed Charlemagne in the eighteenth century and knew nothing of *Othello* at some second-rate college? No, they were at Harvard, where the speaker, Charles Hall Grandgent, was a leading Italian scholar.

We cannot know if Grangent was exaggerating, but the overwhelming testimony of professors at this time suggests that gross ignorance and unabashed anti-intellectualism were not simply widespread but almost obligatory. The anti-intellectualism of college life comes across vividly in early college novels such as Owen Wister's *Philosophy Four* (1904) and Owen Johnson's *Stover at Yale* (1911), in which the serious students are treated by their classmates as eccentric and unpopular grinds. So blatant was the hostility to students who applied themselves to their studies in this period that, as Horowitz points out, these students were called "outsiders." Nor do things seem to have improved greatly by the mid-1930s, when Robert Maynard Hutchins of the University of Chicago observed that the average liberal arts degree "seems to certify that the student has passed an uneventful period without violating any local, state, or federal law, and that he has a fair, if temporary, recollection of what his teachers have said to him."[3]

In the light of such facts, it may not be farfetched to think that today's reports of student prowess in decline are reflecting a recently elevated set of expectations. I have no statistics to prove it, but I suspect that the expectation of serious study from the entire student body dates from the end of World War II, when the standard of academic seriousness was raised by veterans matriculating on the GI Bill and when inexpensive paperback editions made a much wider range of culture available for classroom use. In fact, it is possible that today's college students are *more* committed to their studies than any previous generation, even that of the fifties. In *Coming of Age in New Jersey,* anthropologist Michael Moffatt, who moved into a Rutgers university dormitory in order to study undergraduate life, writes that while "American undergraduates have always had creative ways of getting through college with as little work as possible, . . . they did not all work hard back in the good old days. . . . In fact, they may well work harder in the late twentieth century than they did in the past, for there is now more vocational pressure on them to get good grades than there once was."[4] Even the grade inflation of the last few decades is as much a sign of increasing pressures as of lowered standards.

Not only are the economic pressures to succeed notoriously greater now than they were even in the fifties, but the perennial anti-intellectualism of college life, which remained still powerful in the fifties, has come under increasing criticism as an information-based economy has raised the prestige of intellectual work. A good deal of that anti-intellectualism has returned with a vengeance in the Reagan-Bush era, but it tends to be more on the defensive than it was prior to the sixties. Today's student intellectual is more likely to be labeled an insider than an outsider, and even students prone to anti-intellectualism often betray an ambivalent fascination with the intellectual life. Recent critiques of education notwithstanding, Moffatt found that students themselves believe they are learning things of importance.[5]

At the same time it would be a mistake to deny that as the demographic base of the student body has widened over recent decades, and as the intellectual content of the curriculum has become more diverse and complex, many students no doubt do arrive in college less prepared for academic work than in the past. In *Lives on the Boundary,* Mike Rose argues that while our educational crisis reports are right in pointing up this unpreparedness, these reports focus "too narrowly on test scores and tallies of error" and lack "careful analysis of the students' histories" and "the cognitive and social demands" made by the kind of academic culture students now face.[6] The expansion of the student body to include larger numbers of students from non-traditional backgrounds (a process still far from completion) has been taking place at the very moment when the academic disciplines have become more wide-ranging and less restricted by their traditional definitions.

To put it another way, college students are expected to traverse the vast differences between the different disciplines at the very moment that they must adjust to the even vaster distance between their inherited backgrounds and intellectual culture in general. As Rose comments, these students often come to the university able to "give back what a teacher said in a straightforward lecture. But they have considerable trouble with what has come to be called critical literacy: framing an argument or taking someone else's argument apart, systematically inspecting a document, an issue, or an event, synthesizing different points of view, applying a theory to disparate phenomena, and so on."[7] Rose observes that the authors of the crisis reports get "tremendously distressed about students' difficulties with such tasks, but it is important to remember that, traditionally, such abilities have only been developed in an elite. . . . Ours is the first society in history to expect so many of its people to be able to perform these very sophisticated literacy activities."[8] Finally, Rose points out that the college curriculum is not based on a careful thinking through of the cognitive difficulties such students have in processing the strange culture of the academy. The confusion students feel when exposed to abrupt and unexplained discrepancies in assumptions as they move from course to course and subject to subject takes a special toll on those from minority groups.

Ambivalence about Intellectuals

THE left / right polarization of the culture war has obscured this other important polarity, the one between intellectuals and non-intellectuals, or between those who have been socialized into the intellectual community and those who have not and are not sure they want to be. There is inevitably something invidious about distinctions between "intellectuals" and "nonintellectuals" (and kindred ones between "academics" and "nonacademics," "insiders" and "outsiders," "professional" and "lay" people, etc.), distinctions that are rife with class snobbery and condescension on both sides. Yet the very invidiousness of such distinctions is a reason why we need to confront them, especially in addressing students' problems, for these often have less to do with a lack of knowledge, skills, or "cultural literacy" than with ambivalence about becoming an intellectual, the sort of stuck-up person who knows a lot. As a candid student once said to me, "I'm just not sure how far I want to get into this life of the mind stuff."

Today's ideological divisions are so deep and antagonistic that it is easy to overlook the plight of this student. The gulf is so vast between today's traditionalists and revisionists that the parties seem not to be inhabiting the same intellectual universe. However, as I have noted several times now, to the struggling student who has not been socialized into the discourse of literary criticism, the difference between the traditionalist and the revisionist will seem far less significant than it does to these antagonists themselves. To that student, the traditionalist and the revisionist will seem far more similar to each other than they seem to him, his parents, and his peers. However deep their ideological antagonism, to that student they will still be just a couple of professors speaking a language light-years from his own about problems he has a hard time regarding as problems.

For students estranged from "life of the mind stuff," going from a traditionalist class to a revisionist one can easily seem like the same old thing in a new package. Indeed, the very issues that provoke the traditionalist and the revisionist to attack each other so vigorously constitute a bond that puts them in another world from that student.

Both the difficulties and the promise of this situation were brought home to me several years ago when I was invited to appear on "The Oprah Winfrey Show" to debate Allan Bloom, whose *Closing of the American Mind* was still on the best-seller lists. I am no friend to the Allan Bloom view of education, but once I began to visualize myself debating Bloom before the "Oprah" audience I was forced to think of him less as an ideological enemy than as a fellow intellectual in a common predicament: how to clarify a debate about relativism, nihilism, and other abstractions not commonly presented on daytime network TV.

I had a forewarning of the problem when one of the staffers in charge of briefing the show's guests called me aside and asked me if I could explain to her just what Bloom's book was all about. Oprah and her staff were clearly baffled by Bloom's heavy references to German metaphysics and ancient philosophical quarrels. At the same time there was clearly a genuine curiosity about important educational issues on their part and that of the studio audience. The "debate" never quite got off the ground, but this may have been as much Bloom's and my fault as any-

one's. It is tempting to use the supposed philistinism of the public as an excuse for not working harder to make academic issues
accessible.

The huge sale of Bloom's book and the fact that it was a topic
on "Oprah" should have been reason enough for not underrating
the audience's potential interest in its concerns. Americans may
be suspicious of intellectuals, but they also envy them and are
not disappointed when their children grow up like them. Insofar
as this love-hate relation to life of the mind stuff is inherited by
students, we teachers face complicated combinations of emula-
tion and resistance, attraction and repulsion, to what we have to
purvey. Unless this ambivalence is recognized, there is a certain
irrelevance in the debate over the literary canon.

The Limits of the Canon Debate

FOR that debate could be settled tomorrow without materially
affecting the student who expressed his reservations to me, since
his problem is not with some particular set of books and ideas
but with books and ideas as such. To be sure, his problem can
never be wholly separated from *which* books and ideas these are.
No flesh-and-blood student struggles with a generic book or
idea "as such," only with Plato's *Phaedrus,* Shakespeare's *Othello,*
or Ellison's *Invisible Man,* and it always makes a difference which
particular books and ideas are taught. This is all the more the
case with students so alienated from traditional book culture
that they cannot read the traditional selections at all. Even the
sternest traditionalist will usually concede that it is foolish to
refuse to teach *any* book, however noncanonical, if it figures to
interest a student who otherwise would not read at all.

Yet the attempt to improve education simply by changing the
reading list has a poor track record. For as I suggested in my last
chapter, most of the problems students encounter in the academy lie not in the kinds of texts being read—whether they are

canonical, noncanonical, or what you will—but in the peculiarly analytical ways in which the academy expects students to read and talk about all texts, regardless of their cultural standing. As crucial as it may be to diversify the canon for reasons of cultural and intellectual breadth, such diversification in the past has usually had disappointingly little impact on the more intransigent educational problems. Exclusive preoccupation with the canon—whether in the interest of revising it, keeping it as it is, or returning it to past glories—has too often been a way of avoiding a serious examination of these problems.

In today's canon battle we have been unwittingly replaying an oft-repeated scene. A century ago diehard defenders of the classical Greek and Latin curriculum predicted that civilization would crumble if English literature should replace the classical languages at the center of the curriculum. A few decades later, after English literature had replaced the ancient languages and civilization did not crumble, Anglophiles issued the same dire warnings against new upstarts who wanted to teach the barbaric trash that was presumptuously starting to call itself "American literature." This phrase, said the Anglophiles, was clearly a contradiction in terms, for anyone with taste knew that the few works of any merit written in the United States constituted at best a minor rivulet of the great stream of English letters. Still later, after World War II, the same apocalyptic predictions were revived again when enterprising teachers pushed for the inclusion of modern literature—Joyce, Faulkner, Woolf, Hemingway, Proust, and Yeats—in their courses.

In these battles the revisionist side has always enjoyed an edge because it could point to the failure of the traditional canon, however it was defined at the moment, to engage students. What proved decisive in breaking the deadlock was the prospect that the new subject—English literature, American literature, modern literature—would make academic reading more appealing to students. Thus those teachers after World War II who lobbied for the teaching of modern and contemporary texts overcame antiquarian resistance by arguing that it was the cultural remoteness of the older texts that had caused students' difficulties. As a textbook editor put it in 1948, "the literature of the youth's own century is more easily understood by him. He can read it rapidly without being perplexed by historical background or outmoded style."[9]

Of course, traditionalists who sought to hold the line believed it was good for students to be "perplexed" by their academic tasks, indeed the more perplexed the better. Nineteenth-century defenders of Greek and Latin opposed the introduction of Shakespeare and Milton on the ground that such English authors could never be made *hard* enough to replace Homer and Virgil in the original languages. If this substitution were accepted, they warned, all discipline would go by the boards. The same objection was mounted against the introduction of modern and contemporary literature. Writers like Faulkner and Hemingway lacked high seriousness, it was said, and they were often obscene to boot. We hear the same objections today to the study of the mass media and popular culture.

Those who opposed new subjects for not being hard enough have always lost these battles, however, and one reason is their failure to understand that the difficulty of a text is determined by other factors besides its antiquity or its ranking on a status hierarchy. Teachers soon discovered that the trouble their students had in reading Shakespeare did not disappear when they were given Conrad, Dreiser, or Hemingway. The problem of what the above-quoted educator calls "historical background" does not evaporate just because the work is closer to the student in time, for the historical and cultural context of a contemporary work is not necessarily familiar or easy to formulate. William Faulkner's Yoknapatawpha County or James Joyce's Ireland are not more recognizable or intelligible to the average student than Shakespeare's England. And if the "outmoded style" of Milton and Shakespeare poses problems for students, so does the experimental style of Faulkner, Joyce, and Woolf. Insofar as modern literature is relentlessly symbolic, it requires precisely that digging after hidden meanings that we have seen students and others find so intimidating. Whether the work is by Chaucer or Hemingway, the student still has to speak and write about it in a literary critical language that must be learned.

For these reasons, canon revision has never quite lived up to its expectations. Once the battle is won to teach the heretofore excluded texts, the chronic learning problems tend to reappear. This difficulty has been largely ignored by educational progressives, who are often too quick to blame student alienation from academic literacy on the elitist or conservative aspects of that literacy. The uncomfortable truth is that students can be just as alienated from populist forms of academic literacy as from conservative ones. If looking for hidden meanings is something you are not used to doing, looking for them in *The Color Purple* will seem as strange as looking for them in *Hamlet*.

The Fear of Decreasing Difficulty and the View from the Back Bench

IF it is tempting for progressives to exaggerate the educational benefits of canon revision, it is equally tempting for traditionalists to exaggerate the extent to which canon revision will make things easy for students. Here lies the fallacy in the widely held belief that introducing noncanonical works into the curriculum makes academic study less rigorous, levels the distinction between classics and comic books, and panders to student self-indulgence.

The fact is, with the world of knowledge becoming increasingly larger and more complex, the last thing anyone needs to fear is that the study of culture will become too easy. The seductive assumption, however, is that only certain classics possess enough substance to justify being studied. Everything else is assumed simply to lack the sort of "meaning" necessary to sustain serious academic analysis. This fear that difficulty is vanishing is expressed by NEH Chairman Lynne V. Cheney, who writes of an educational "Gresham's law" whereby "the easy and entertaining" drive out "the hard and the challenging. Teachers teach popular novels and slasher films instead of Charlotte Brontë and Shakespeare."[10]

Cheney does not feel the need to defend the proposition that popular novels and slasher films are *necessarily* "easy and entertaining." I seriously doubt that slasher films are very frequently taught, much less taught as "entertaining," and it is not so long ago that Brontë and Shakespeare themselves were thought too easy and entertaining to be worth teaching. Since believers in the unique difficulty of the classics are rarely aware how recently their favorites became classics, they can readily update the list of approved texts without worrying about the fact that those favorites were often considered popular rubbish a generation ago and in some quarters still are. A recent editorial bemoaning the "travesty of scholarship" represented by the teaching of popular culture asserts that "Bart Simpson isn't Tom Joad of 'The Grapes of Wrath' "—as if Steinbeck's dated social realism were universally admired, when in fact, for many teachers past and present it would be an example of popular vulgarity.[11]

A clue to the logic underlying the fear of vanishing difficulty appears in a recent *Chicago Tribune* article, whose writer deplores the introduction of popular music, television, and film into academic courses:

> Anyone who has stood at a podium recognizes that all classrooms have the same topography: Seated down front are the few students who share their teacher's enthusiasm, while the back rows are inhabited by the majority, who virtually dare the instructor to force some culture down their throats. But if all books are equal, that resistance can be overcome simply by reducing the syllabus to the tastes of those back-benchers.[12]

At least this comment allows a glimpse of academic reality to peep through its misconceptions: The stark division between the enthusiastic front-bench minority and the disaffected back-bench majority is indeed a persistent feature of classroom life. And it is true, as I have noted, that revisions in the syllabus have often been motivated by the hope that the back-bench students who are left cold by the classics will be more responsive to texts presumably closer to their interests. What is not true is that the introduction of popular texts and subjects ends up making things easier for the backbenchers.

To see why it does not, we need only look at an example of academic popular culture discourse. In his book *No Respect: Intellectuals and Popular Culture,* Andrew Ross, one of the most intelligent current analysts of popular culture, writes about how gay culture has appropriated certain images from ostensibly heterosexual films of the thirties and forties:

> . . . there is no guarantee that what is *encoded* in these film scenarios will be *decoded* in the same way by different social groups with different sexual orientations. This is nowhere more obvious than in the highly developed gay subculture that evolved around a fascination with classical Hollywood film and, in particular, with film stars like Judy Garland, Bette Davis, Mae West, Greta Garbo, Marlene Dietrich, Joan Crawford. . . . Denied the possibility of "masculine" and "feminine" positions of spectatorship, and excluded by conventional representations of male-as-hero or narrative agent, . . . the lived spectatorship of gay and lesbian subcultures is expressed largely through imaginary or displaced relations to the straight meanings of these images and discourses of a parent culture.[13]

The sophistication and range of reference here would be as difficult for students to assimilate and reproduce as any traditional critical interpretation of Shakespeare or Dickens. If pure difficulty is the only issue, a popular film or romance can be made as taxing to study as any other work.

For what creates difficulty—and here is the point I have been driving at—is not just the object of study but *the kind of question being asked about it.* There is no functional connection between the status level of a text (however this may be measured) and the degree of complexity or difficulty attained by the interpretation of it for some hypothetical average reader. The word "the" becomes difficult when its historical development and grammar are studied by philologists or linguists, and a paper clip could be made difficult by being studied in relation to the history of metals or technology. By the same token, it does not follow that culturally acknowledged great works generate a more substantial, challenging, and interesting critical or pedagogical discourse than do less valued works.

A neo-Marxist analysis of Vanna White's autobiography, *Vanna Speaks,* one that emphasized, say, the commodification of the self under postmodern capitalism, might be more challenging than any number of analyses of weightier tomes than Vanna's. The average scholarly article on *King Lear* or *War and Peace* is not in and of itself necessarily more interesting or rewarding than the average scholarly article on the dime novel or the semiotics of advertising. In fact, very little Shakespeare criticism packs the intellectual power of George Orwell's essays on British boys' weeklies, smutty penny postcards, and cheap detective novels— something which no doubt explains why these Orwell essays appear so frequently in freshman anthologies while the ones on Shakespeare do not.[14] Nor is this a case of Orwell's genius triumphing over trivial subject matter, except in the sense that it took genius for Orwell to see how far from trivial such subject matter could be if one asked the right kinds of cultural questions about it.

From the vantage point of the back bench, an examination question that asks for a discussion of the cultural significance of a Harlequin romance will be no snap. On the contrary, a question on the Harlequin may actually prove *more* difficult than a standard question on a literary classic, since there is not the fund of stereotyped critical observations that students can draw on for such ephemeral writing as there is for the classics. Then, too, because students, like their teachers, have been conditioned to think that only high cultural works possess hidden meaning, they are likely to be perplexed when asked to look for such meaning in a Harlequin or a clothing ad.

A common objection is that since students are *already* bombarded by popular culture in their everyday lives, it is superfluous or perverse to ask them to study it in courses. Like other specious arguments about popular culture, this one fails to distinguish between studying a cultural form and uncritically taking it in. This confusion is evidently peculiar to the humanities. No one accuses criminologists of promoting crime because they make criminal behavior an object of academic study, but because the humanities often study culturally precious objects and traditions, the misconception arises that studying a subject constitutes an endorsement of it and its view of the world. Even if those who say that popular culture is mindless and degraded are right, this is an argument *for* studying that culture rather than for neglecting it. After all, how something so mindless and degraded could have become such a powerful force in our lives cries out for investigation.[15]

Far from being a threat to high culture, however, the study of popular culture seems necessary if students are to grasp the significance of the "high" versus the "popular" distinction and the value judgments that go along with it. Such comparative study, in fact, was recommended by the great traditionalist critic F. R. Leavis, who urged the incorporation of popular culture into English studies—a fact forgotten by the neoconservatives who invoke his authority against current trends. As Leavis put it, "a serious concern for education in reading cannot stop at reading. Practical criticism of literature must be associated with training in awareness of the environment—advertising, the cinema, the press, architecture, and so on, for, clearly, to the pervasive influence of this environment the literary training of sensibility in school is an inadequate reply."[16] Leavis recognized that academic high culture could not "reply" to the advance of popular culture unless it extended diplomatic recognition to the adversary. Obviously he did not think that the study of popular culture would make things any easier for students.

Complicating and "problematizing" are the characteristic activity of the academy, which takes things that ostensibly, from the commonsense point of view, seem simple and uncontroversial—a literary classic, a war, an election, an epidemic, a comic strip—and shows that they are complex, problematic, less stable and self-evident than we thought. This ethos of difficulty is reflected in the conventions of the academic article, which characteristically opens with a declaration that topic X is thought to be unproblematic and transparent and then proceeds to reveal hitherto unnoticed difficulties and complications. The academy makes every subject, no matter how apparently transparent, seem hard.

But of course, to defend the humanities against the charge that they have not been making things hard enough is only to open them to the opposing charge that they make things all too hard, making literature so needlessly complicated and obscure that its simple and innocent appeal is vitiated. Caught in the middle of our cultural ambivalence about intellectuality, the humanities are damned if they do and damned if they don't: If they open reading lists to noncanonical texts, they are accused of robbing the humanities of their intellectual challenge, but if they teach canonical or noncanonical texts in ways that threaten commonsense interpretations, they are accused of taking those texts away from common readers and making them the possession of an elite coterie. (Attacks on literary theory epitomize this contradictory logic: Academic theory is blamed for turning teachers at once into crudely doctrinaire activists and into coldly intellectual obscurantists.)

Thus not everyone will be impressed by the critic just quoted who makes Hollywood films challenging by pointing out how gay culture has appropriated them. We want academic subjects to be challenging, but not if it means transgressing majority beliefs. In a speech several years ago on the public role of the National Endowment for the Humanities, then-Chairman Edward Curran spoke of "the failure of scholars and research-oriented professors to introduce students and the public to the simple, natural appeal that these disciplines [the humanities] have held for ages. . . ."[17] As I noted earlier, this position has virtually become the official line of the NEH under the current chairman, Lynne V. Cheney, who, even as she complains that the humanities are being made too easy by the infusion of inferior works, defends those same humanities as a repository of uncomplicated truths about "what it means to be human."

We begin to see the built-in conflict between the academy's commitment to complication and difficulty and the public's need for programmatic reduction. The conflict is reproduced in the tension between academic writing, in which the pressure is to leave no complication unexplored, and journalism, in which the pressure is to reduce and simplify to the bottom line. The culture war has exposed the huge gulf between these kinds of writing, but it has also exposed the new convergence of their interests. If journalists have come into conflict with humanists, it is because those humanists are no longer content to serve an exclusively antiquarian function and have begun to compete with journalists as interpreters of contemporary life.

The critic Gregory Jay has argued that a dialogue needs to be established between the media and the academy through joint meetings and conferences. Jay suggests that contact with media people would help academics express themselves more clearly to students and the larger public, while "the media could use a few lessons from the deconstructionists," who have developed "methods for taking apart the prefabricated representation of truth."[18] It is an idea that could be adapted to teaching through joint courses involving the humanities and journalism departments. It has long been something of a scandal that the teaching of composition in English departments is usually isolated from the teaching of journalism. Increased interchange between academics and journalists, and between humanities and journalism departments, would figure to benefit both academic and journalistic writing by challenging their different kinds of self-serving justification. Academics would get away less easily with saying, in effect, "It's just too complicated for you to understand, so don't expect me to explain," and journalists would be less prone to say, "Academic complication is always bogus, so I needn't bother to understand."

With luck, a result of the culture war will be to help journalists become more complicated and academics more accessible, even as each becomes less prone to preach to the already converted in their different audiences. This in turn could make the transition from reading the newspaper to reading academic writing less jarring for students. Students may then find it easier to see that life of the mind stuff exists everywhere, not just in school, and that it is not as scary as they thought.

Chapter 6

Other Voices, Other Rooms

AN undergraduate tells of an art history course in which the instructor observed one day, "As we now know, the idea that knowledge can be objective is a positivist myth that has been exploded by postmodern thought." It so happens the student is concurrently enrolled in a political science course in which the instructor speaks confidently about the objectivity of his discipline as if it had not been "exploded" at all. What do you do? the student is asked. "What else can I do?" he says. "I trash objectivity in art history, and I presuppose it in political science."

A second undergraduate describes a history teacher who makes a point of stressing the superiority of Western culture in developing the ideas of freedom, democracy, and free market capitalism that the rest of the world is now rushing to imitate. She also has a literature teacher who describes such claims of Western supremacy as an example of the hegemonic ideology by which the United States arrogates the right to police the world. When asked which course she prefers, she replies, "Well, I'm getting an A in both."

To some of us these days, the moral of these stories would be that students have become cynical relativists who care less about convictions than about grades and careers. In fact, if anything is surprising, it is that more students do not behave in this cynical fashion, for the established curriculum encourages it. The disjunction of the curriculum is a far more powerful source of relativism than any doctrine preached by the faculty.

One of the oddest things about the university is that it calls itself a community of scholars yet organizes its curriculum in a way that conceals the links of the community from those who are not already aware of them. The courses being given at any moment on a campus represent any number of rich potential conversations within and across the disciplines. But since students experience these conversations only as a series of monologues, the conversations become actual only for the minority who can reconstruct them on their own. No self-respecting educator would deliberately design a system guaranteed to keep students dependent on the whim of the individual instructor. Yet this is precisely the effect of a curriculum composed of courses that are not in dialogue with one another.

Ships in the Night

THE problem deepens when teachers are further apart. A student today can go from a course in which the universality of Western culture is taken for granted (and therefore not articulated) to a course in which it is taken for granted (and therefore not articulated) that such claims of universality are fallacious and deceptive. True, for the best students the resulting cognitive dissonance is no great problem. The chance to try on a variety of clashing ideas, to see what they feel like, is one of the most exciting opportunities an education can provide; it can be especially rewarding for students who come to the university with already developed skills at summarizing and weighing arguments and synthesizing conflicting positions on their own. Many students, however, become confused or indifferent and react as the above two students did by giving their teachers whatever they seem to want even though it is contradictory.

Then, too, when their teachers' conflicting perspectives do not enter into a common discussion, students may not even be able to infer what is wanted. Like everyone else, teachers tend to betray their crucial assumptions as much in what they do *not* say, what they take to go without saying, as in what they say explicitly. To students who are not at home in the academic intellectual community, the significance of these silences and exclusions is likely to be intimidating, if it does not elude them entirely.

Furthermore, in an academic environment in which there is increasingly less unspoken common ground, it may not even be clear to students that their teachers are in conflict, for different words may be used by several teachers for the same concepts or the same words for different concepts. If students do not know that "positivism" has in some quarters become a derogatory buzzword for any belief in objectivity, they may not become aware that the art history and political science teachers in the above example are in disagreement. A student who goes from one humanist who speaks of "traditional moral themes" to another who speaks of "patriarchal discursive practices" may not become aware that the two teachers are actually referring to the same thing. Students in such cases are being exposed to some of the major cultural debates of their time, but in a way that makes it difficult to recognize them *as* debates.

Note, too, that the instructors in these situations are protected by the insularity of their classrooms, which makes it unnecessary, if not impossible, for them to confront the challenges to their assumptions that would be represented by their colleagues. Professors do not expect such immunity from peer criticism when they publish their work or appear at professional conferences. It is only in the classroom that such immunity is taken for granted as if it were a form of academic freedom. Since students enjoy no such protection, one can hardly blame them if they, too, protect themselves by compartmentalizing the contradictions to which they are exposed, as my first student did when he became an objectivist in one course and an antiobjectivist in the other.

I recall a semester late in college when I took a course in modern poetry taught by a New Critic, a follower of T. S. Eliot, and a course in seventeenth-century English literature taught by an older scholar who resented Eliot and the New Critics, who had attacked John Milton for his grandiloquence and lack of irony. Three days a week between ten and eleven I listened with dutiful respect to the New Critic's theories of irony and paradox, and between eleven and twelve I listened with dutiful respect to the argument that these New Critical theories had no application whatsoever to Milton, Dryden, and their contemporaries. What was really odd, however, is that I hardly focused at the time on the fact that my two teachers were in disagreement.

Was I just ridiculously slow to comprehend the critical issues that were at stake? Perhaps so, but since no one was asking me to think about the relationship between the two courses, I did not. If my teachers disagreed, this was their business—a professional dispute that did not concern me. Each course was challenging enough on its own terms, and to have raised the question of how they related would have only risked needlessly multiplying difficulties for myself. Then, too, for me to ask my teachers about their differences might have seemed impertinent and ill mannered—who was I to impugn their authority? Only later did it dawn on me that studying different centuries and clashing theories without having them brought together had made things much *harder* since it removed the element of contrast.

Contrast is fundamental to understanding, for no subject, idea, or text is an island. In order to become intelligible "in itself," it needs to be seen in its relation to other subjects, ideas, and texts. When this relation of interdependence is obscured because different courses do not communicate, subjects, ideas, and texts become harder to comprehend, if not unintelligible. We think we are making things simpler for students by abstracting periods, texts, and authors from their relationships with other periods, texts, and authors so that we can study them closely in a purified space. But the very act of isolating an object from its contrasting background and relations makes it hard to grasp. Since we cannot talk about everything all at once, subjects do have to be distinguished and to that extent isolated from one another. But this isolation does not have to preclude connections and relations. It is hard to grasp the modernity of modern literature unless one can compare it with something that is not modern.

That is why teachers in modern periods need nonmodernists (and vice versa) in order to make their subjects intelligible to their students, just as teachers who defend the culture of the West need the teachers who criticize it (and vice versa). Without the criticisms, after all, there would be no need to defend the West to begin with. Insofar as neither a defense nor a critique of tradition makes sense apart from the dialogue these positions are engaged in, a curriculum which removes that dialogue from view defeats the goals of traditionalists and revisionists alike. It is true that fundamental conflicts like these may turn out to be nonnegotiable. But no one knows this in advance, and even if a dispute proves to be nonnegotiable, to learn that this is the case is not worthless.

I noted earlier that among the factors that make academic culture more confusing today than in the past is not only that there is more controversy but that there is even controversy about what can legitimately be considered controversial. Traditionalists are often angry that there should even *be* a debate over the canon, while revisionists are often angry that there should even be a debate over "political correctness," or the relevance of ideology and politics to their subjects. A recent feminist critic says she finds it "astonishing" that it still needs repeating at this late date that "the perspective assumed to be 'universal' which has dominated knowledge . . . has actually been male and culture-bound."[1] Since the feminist argument, however, is that we still fail to see how culture-bound our thinking is, it is hard to see why this critic should be astonished that she still needs to make the point. Another political critic writes that "we are perhaps already weary of the avalanche of papers, books, and conferences entitled 'The Politics of X,' and we have recently begun to question that most hallowed of all political slogans on the left, 'everything is political.' "[2] Yet the idea of politics that this critic and her audience are already "weary of" is one that most people have not yet encountered and might well find incomprehensible. The "advanced" academic and the layperson (or the traditional academic) are so far apart that what is already old news to one has not yet become intelligible to the other.

Imagine how this affects students who, at the moment they are negotiating the difficult transition from the lay culture to the academic culture, must also negotiate the unpredictable and unfathomable discrepancies between academic departments and factions. When there is no correlation of the different discourses to which students are exposed, it becomes especially difficult for them to infer which assumptions are safe and which are likely to be challenged. The problem is that knowledge of what is and is not considered potentially or legitimately controversial cannot be learned a priori; you cannot get it out of E. D. Hirsch's *Dictionary of Cultural Literacy*. Such knowledge comes only through interaction with a community, and that interaction is precisely what is prevented by a disconnected system of courses. Then, too, assumptions about what is and is not potentially controversial tend to change from one moment to the next and one sub-community to the next, and they are changing at a faster rate today than in the past.

Thomas S. Kuhn in *The Structure of Scientific Revolutions* describes moments of crisis or "paradigm shift" in the sciences, when "a law that cannot even be demonstrated to one group of scientists may . . . seem intuitively obvious to another."[3] The fate of Kuhn's own book is an interesting case in point. Even as his sociological account of scientific paradigm change has been treated as virtual holy writ by many literary theorists (for a while it seemed almost obligatory to begin every book or essay with a respectful bow to Kuhn), his work has often been ignored or dismissed by scientists and philosophers of science, who accuse him of subverting the concept of objective truth in reducing scientific discovery to "mob psychology." As the controversy over Kuhn has revealed, both the literati and the scientists have remained largely walled up within their clashing assumptions about objectivity, the smugness of which might have been punctured had these parties been forced to argue with each other in their teaching. This mutual smugness has persisted in the sniper fire that continues to be exchanged over the concept of objectivity and the extent to which knowledge is independent of the social situation of the knower; revisionists sneer at the concept and traditionalists sneer at the very idea of questioning it.

The question neither group seems to ask is what it must be like to be a student caught in the crossfire between these conflicting views of objectivity, each one prone to present itself as "intuitively obvious" and uncontroversial. A rhetoric scholar, Gregory Colomb, has studied the disorientation experienced by a bright high school graduate who, after doing well in a humanities course as a freshman at the University of Chicago, tried to apply her mastery to a social science course, only to come up with a grade of C.[4] Imagine trying to write an academic paper when you sense that almost anything you say can be used against you and that the intellectual moves that got you an A in existentialist philosophy may get you a C minus and a dirty look in Skinnerian behaviorism.

Consider the fact that the passive voice that is so standard in sociology writing ("it will be contended in this paper . . .") has been perennially rebuked in English courses.[5] Or consider something so apparently trivial as the convention of using the present tense to describe actions in literature and philosophy and the past tense to describe them in history. Plato *says* things in literary and philosophical accounts while in historical accounts he *said* them. Experienced writers become so accustomed to such tense shifting that it seems a simple matter, but it reflects deep-rooted and potentially controversial differences between disciplines. Presumably, Plato speaks in the present in literary and philosophical contexts because ideas there are considered time-less; only when we move over to history does it start to matter that the writer is dead.[6] We English teachers write "tense shift" in the margin when student writers betray uncertainty about this convention, but how do we expect them to "get" it when they pass from the very different time zones of history and philosophy / English with no engagement of the underlying issues?

One of the most frequent comments teachers make on student papers is "What's your evidence?" But nobody would ever finish a piece of writing if it were necessary to supply evidence for everything being said, so in order to write, one must acquire a sense of which statements have to be supported by evidence (or further argument) and which ones a writer can get away with because they are already taken for granted by the imagined audience. What happens, then, when a writer has no way of knowing whether an assumption that he or she got away with with audience A will also be conceded by audience B? It is no wonder that students protect themselves from the insecurity of such a situation by "psyching out" each course as it comes—and then forgetting about it as soon as possible after the final exam in order to clear their minds for the seemingly unrelated demands of the next set of courses.

It is not only ideas and reasoning processess but the recall of basic information as well that figure to be impaired by disjunctive curricular organization. To use the jargon of information theory, an information system that is experienced as an unrelated series of signals will be weak in the kind of redundancy that is needed for information to be retained. Faced with a curriculum overloaded with data and weak in redundancy, students may find it difficult to know which items of information they are supposed to remember. Then, too, a student may be exposed to the same information in several courses while failing to recognize it as "the same," since it is contextualized differently in each course. When students fail to identify a cultural literacy item on a test, the problem may be not that they don't know the information but that they don't know they know it; they may have learned it in a context whose relevance to the test question they don't recognize. What is learned seems so specific to a particular course that it is difficult for students to see its application beyond.

The critic Kenneth Burke once compared the intellectual life of a culture to a parlor in which different guests are forever dropping in and out. As the standard curriculum represents the intellectual life, however, there is no parlor; the hosts congregate in separate rooms with their acolytes and keep their differences and agreements to themselves. Making one's way through the standard curriculum is rather like trying to comprehend a phone conversation by listening at only one end.[7] You can manage it up to a point, but this is hardly the ideal way to do it.

To venture a final comparison, it is as if you were to try to learn the game of baseball by being shown a series of rooms in which you see each component of the game separately: pitchers going through their windups in one room; hitters swinging their bats in the next; then infielders, outfielders, umpires, fans, field announcers, ticket scalpers, broadcasters, hot dog vendors, and so on. You see them all in their different roles, but since you see them separately you get no clear idea of what the game actually looks like or why the players do what they do. No doubt you would come away with a very imperfect understanding of baseball under these conditions. Yet it does not seem farfetched to compare these circumstances with the ones students face when they are exposed to a series of disparate courses, subjects, and

perspectives and expected not only to infer the rules of the aca-
demic-intellectual game but to play it competently themselves.

The Course Fetish

IT is tempting to blame these problems on bad teaching, seemingly rectifiable by encouraging instructors to be more sensitive
to their students' predicament. Certainly more sensitivity on the
part of teachers would help. But even the most sympathetic and
sensitive teacher cannot be sure which of his or her views may
be flatly contradicted by the next teacher encountered by his or
her students. Then, too, though good teaching may have its
inherently individualistic aspects, we all need others at times to
counteract our biases and to make up for our gaps in knowledge. For this reason the problems I have been discussing cannot be effectively addressed at the level of individual teaching.
They are curricular problems, and a curriculum is not simply
the sum total of separate acts of teaching but a systematic organization of teaching. In fact, the habit of reducing all questions
about education to questions about individual *teaching* discourages us from thinking systematically about the curriculum. Our
very use of the term "the classroom" to stand for the entire educational process is a symptom of this constricted way of thinking, which I call the "course fetish," though it might also be
called the "cult of the great teacher."

How well one can teach depends not just on individual virtuosity but on the possibilities and limits imposed by the structure in which one works. It may not hold for everyone, but I
believe I am a better teacher when I am able to take my colleagues as reference points in my classroom. As long as teaching
is viewed as an inherently solo performance, too much is made
to depend on the teacher's personal resources, something which
puts teachers under inordinate pressure and makes for burnout.

Only a weak system would depend on perpetual feats of personal virtuosity to keep it functioning at its best.

This point has been made by a powerful critic of the course system, Joseph Tussman, a reformer who helped develop an experimental program at the University of California at Berkeley that I shall be looking at in my final chapter. In a book on the program published in 1969, Tussman pointed out that the course system had become so pervasive "that we have come to regard the conditions of course teaching as the conditions of teaching in general." He argued that the problem with the course system is that since "the courses are generally unrelated and competitive, . . . each professor knows that he has a valid claim to only a small fraction of the student's time and attention. The effect is that no teacher is in a position to be responsible for, or effectively concerned with, the student's total educational situation. The student presents himself to the teacher in fragments, and not even the advising system can put him back together again." These limiting conditions, noted Tussman, are ones "of which every sensitive teacher is bitterly aware. But there is nothing he can do about it. He can develop a coherent course, but a collection of coherent courses may be simply an incoherent collection."[8]

As Tussman maintained, the only effective unit for educational planning is the *program,* not the course. We tend, however, to associate programs and systems with bureaucracy, mechanization, and institutionalization, terms lacking in the sentimental emotional resonance that we attach to the idea of "the classroom" presided over by the great teacher. The magical aura of "the classroom" lies in the illusion that is is not part of a system at all, that it is an island somehow exempt from the incursions of bureaucracy. We know that the truth is otherwise, that courses have to be scheduled, assigned to rooms, listed in the catalog, and assimilated to the grid of credit hours, requirements, and grades. The course, however, is experienced not as an extension of bureaucratic organization but as a force that transcends and redeems bureaucratic organization and makes it tolerable.

This explains why we frequently hear academics speak irreverently about the existence of *departments* but hardly ever about their courses, though the course is an expression of the same process of bureaucratic specialization and privatization that produced the department. The department is thought to epitomize the divisive, competitive, meanly professionalized aspects of academic life. Its existence is a reminder of the arbitrary fences with which each discipline selfishly guards its disciplinary turf, of factional rivalry and a narrowly self-serving and proprietary view of intellectual life. The faculty meeting, an expression of the departmental ethos, typifies this realm of petty strife from which the course is felt to be a saving escape. As Tussman put it, "the faculty meeting—college, departmental, or committee— is the abrasive ordeal from which one flees to the delicious, healing privacy of one's own course."[9]

Whereas the department epitomizes the bureaucratic aspects of academic life, the course does not feel like a bureaucratic entity at all. Thus "the classroom" is believed to be what the university is really all about after we factor out the necessary evils of administration, departments, publish or perish, research, faculty meetings, and even the curriculum itself, which are seen as realms of conflict. This symbolic opposition in all its sentimentality is neatly exemplified in the recent popular film *The Dead Poets Society,* in which a brilliantly creative and eccentric teacher of literature is pitted against a puritanical, repressive, and life-denying prep school administration.

But the most familiar representation of the sentimental image of the course as a scene of conflict-free community is the one presented on untold numbers of college catalog covers: A small, intimate class is sprawled informally on the gently sloping campus greensward, shady trees overhead and ivy-covered buildings in the background. Ringed in a casual semicircle, the students gaze with rapt attention at a teacher who is reading aloud from

a small book—a volume of poetry, we inevitably assume, probably Keats or Dickinson or Whitman. The classroom, in these
images, is a garden occupying a redemptive space inside the
bureaucratic and professional machine. It is a realm of unity and
presence in a world otherwise given over to endless difference,
conflict, competition, and factionalism. The classroom resem-
bles the primitive Protestant Church, freed from the ecclesias-
tical externals that only tend to intervene between the believer
and the authentic experience of the sacred texts. The curriculum, by contrast, is identified with the bureaucratic machine
and is represented in the catalog not in pastoral images but in
mechanically numbered lists of departments, courses, and
requirements, although the cold linearity of this organization in
its own way obscures the conflicts between departments and
courses.

To the extent that the curriculum is associated with alien
bureaucracy, the course fetish carries with it a certain disbelief
in the very need for a curriculum. Underlying the course fetish
finally is a conviction (as I recently heard a prominent philosopher and educational theorist say) that there is nothing wrong
with today's education that cannot be cured by getting good
teachers together and simply turning them loose. And there is a
certain truth to this view. No doubt the best things that happen
in universities *are* the things that happen in "the classroom." But
the romance of "the classroom" blinds us to the steep educational price we pay when classrooms are isolated from one another.

"The classroom" embodies a contradiction: In the process of
creating one kind of community it thwarts the community that
it could be constituting with other courses.[10] For students, this
results in the effects of cognitive dissonance that I described at
the beginning of this chapter. For faculty as well as students it
results in a stifling lack of intellectual community. It is not surprising that professors flock in increasing numbers to professional conferences and symposia, where they find the kind of
collegial discussion that rarely occurs at home. No wonder they

feel a lack of community at home when they spend so much of their time there isolated from one another in their courses.

To say this, to be sure, is to go against the widespread belief that professors now spend all too *little* of their time in their courses. This is sometimes indeed the case—though I think far less commonly than is thought. The more fundamental question we should be asking in most cases is not *how much* time teachers are spending in the classroom but *under what conditions.* Spending adequate time in the classroom is obviously crucial, but that time would be spent less wastefully if each classroom were not off limits to other classrooms, if classrooms formed a conversation instead of a set of ships passing in the night.

The Cafeteria or the Food?

MY argument is only a new twist to a complaint about curricular fragmentation that has been persistent since the beginnings of mass education: that the curriculum has become a cafeteria counter, a smorgasbord, a department store, a garage sale—pick your favorite figure of speech. This complaint, found everywhere in the writings of today's popular critics of education, is based on the accurate perception that students have trouble making sense of the disparate and clashing materials with which the curriculum bombards them. Unfortunately the reasonable observation that the curriculum is a mere cafeteria counter tends to get mixed up with far more dubious misgivings about the curriculum's *components.*

That is, the popular educational critics tend to be upset about so many different aspects of education that they fail to stick long enough with the part of their diagnosis that we might be able to agree on and actually do something about. It is one thing to object that the curriculum has become a cafeteria counter and quite another to object that the food is poisoned.

In *The Closing of the American Mind,* for example, Allan Bloom writes that today's student is confronted with "a bewildering variety of courses," with "no official guidance, no university-wide agreement about what he *should* study."[11] He continues:

> Each department or great division of the university makes a pitch for itself, and each offers a course of study that will make the student an initiate. But how to choose among them? How do they relate to one another? The fact is they do not address one another. They are competing and contradictory, without being aware of it. The problem of the whole is urgently indicated by the very existence of the specialties, but it is never systematically posed. The net effect of the student's encounter with the college catalogue is bewilderment and very often demoralization.[12]

Bloom here trenchantly identifies the real confusion students experience going from one unrelated course to the next. But if he is right that the heart of the curricular problem lies in the fact that academic divisions "do not address one another," then one would think that the obvious place to start in redressing the problem would be to find some way to get those divisions to address one another. If curricular disconnection is a big part of the trouble, then before we tinker with anything else, why not connect what is already there and see if it works better?

Unfortunately Bloom never stops to consider the solution his own argument suggests. He cannot, because he assumes that connecting or integrating courses and departments would require "university-wide agreement" about their contents. But you do not have to agree about the relative merits of Shakespeare and Toni Morrison in order to connect Shakespeare and Morrison. You do not have to agree about the status of objectivity or the relation of politics to truth in order to connect the discussions of these questions that are currently taking place in literature, law, sociology, anthropology, religion, economics, philosophy of science, and medicine. The disagreements themselves can be the point of connection.

It never occurs to Bloom that a solution to what he calls the "problem of the whole" of the university might be latent in the clash of "competing and contradictory" perspectives itself—if these perspectives could be made, in his words, to "address one another." True to the long tradition of general education philosophy, he confuses curricular *coherence* with *consensus*. He fails to separate the problem of curricular incoherence, which our opposing factions might combine their efforts to do something about, with all the other things about the university—real and imagined—that he dislikes: relativism, specialization, radical politics, the research fetish, and what you will. No sooner does Bloom identify a problem, curricular disconnection, that we might come together to solve than he confuses this problem with things that would be much harder to change and in some cases are not obviously in need of changing or not fairly described by Bloom: that there is no consensus on what we should be teaching; that academics are overspecialized; that they neglect teaching in favor of research; that sex, relativism, and rock and roll are taking over; that there is too much teaching of the wrong kinds of books or the wrong kind of politics.

Consider Bloom's attack on research specialization, by now such a familiar target that we ignore the fact that in the humanities at least, the charge is no longer self-evidently valid. For a generation now, the academic humanities have actually *penalized* narrow specialization, reserving their highest rewards for work that propounds sweeping cultural theories and broad interdisciplinary generalizations and promises to revise the paradigm for thinking about its subject.[13] In part this change is a response to the tremendous outpouring of criticism of overspecialization since the end of World War II. If the humanities are "over" anything, they are overgeneralized rather than overspecialized; there is too much pressure on younger scholars to be "broad-gauged" and interdisciplinary in order to get teaching positions and then produce major theoretical breakthroughs in order to get tenure. You have only to look at the terms in which books are now promoted by university presses to see that the prestige has shifted from the narrowly positivistic specialized study that was still the staple of scholarship before World War II ("The Passive Voice in Old Icelandic") to the "pathbreaking" general thesis that takes much of culture as its province. That such claims are often four-fifths hype does not alter the fact that a shift in priorities has taken place, a pathbreaking shift, one might even say.

To be sure, humanities research still *looks* as specialized as ever because its paradigm-shattering arguments are still often couched in highly specialized vocabularies. A doctoral dissertation on "The Construction of Gender in the Later Romantic Lyric" thus may seem to operate at the same narrow level of specialization as "The Passive Voice in Old Icelandic." To the lay reader who would find both works opaque, there seems no significant difference. But the claims made by the gender study in its specialized vocabulary are likely to be broad, generalized, and ambitiously political—as Bloom and other critics concede when they attack such work for being *too* ambitiously political. If humanities research were really as specialized as its critics say it is, they would not be so up in arms over its political claims.

What critics like Bloom (and Lynne V. Cheney of the NEH, in report after report attacking humanities specialization) mistake for specialization are, in fact, new languages of generalization whose premises they either do not understand or do not agree with—usually both. These new languages—usually lumped under the term "theory"—have made it possible for disciplines that were once closed to one another by their specialization not only to converse but to poach off one another to a notorious degree, with anthropologists reading literary theorists, literary theorists reading philosophers and social thinkers, and lawyers, literary scholars, and communications studies people holding conferences on subjects like "Interpretation across the Disciplines." Fields that had little basis for talking to one another when "The Passive Voice in Old Icelandic" was the dominant model for a research project now share considerable common ground. A Melville scholar and a Civil War historian are likely to be no longer so locked into their specialized interests that they cannot converse about the connection between slavery and literature. Though they may take opposing sides, these scholars will now tend to be interested in the same general questions like the debate over the social relations of literature.

If no dialogue takes place between the Melville scholar and the Civil War historian, the likely reason today is not that they are too specialized but that they lack an institutional structure in which that dialogue can occur, especially in their undergraduates' hearing. If a kind of "specialization" is still the problem, it is a kind imposed by the fact that they teach in different departments and classrooms rather than anything inherent in the ways they conceive their subjects or do their work. (On the other hand, the physical and curricular separation of these teachers may make it hard for them to see the latent common ground between their disciplines.) The lack of dialogue is the outcome of an antiquated curricular structure which no longer reflects the way academic inquiry is conducted. The course fetish perpetuates specialization even as the disciplines have been moving away from it.

Mike Rose observes that "the American university has yet to figure out, conceptually or institutionally, how to integrate its general education mission with its research mission."[14] In the era when "The Passive Voice in Old Icelandic" was a model research topic, it was virtually impossible to reconcile these missions since there was no way to build a general education course around such a narrow concern. The professor was forced to abandon his specialty when he became an undergraduate teacher, a demand few were able to adapt to very well, or else he inflicted it on unfortunate students. The new emphasis on more generalized kinds of research has made it easier for teachers to adapt their research interests to the needs of general education and undergraduate education, thus overcoming the old split between research and teaching. (It has for some time been an unspoken premise at humanities job interviews that the prospective teacher must be able to adapt his or her dissertation to the needs of a freshman course.)

But it is one thing for individuals to integrate their teaching and research missions and another for universities to do so. The research / teaching split *does* remain a serious problem, but (in the humanities at least) no longer because research is overly specialized, as Bloom and others charge, but because the curriculum as a whole fails to bring out whatever in that research has broadly general interest and make it clear to students and others. Insofar as research is successfully generalized for undergraduates, it is because of the efforts of individual teachers. If my argument here is correct, however, this task requires the collaboration and integration of teachers if it is to be more than intermittently successful.

Instead of ritualistically bemoaning the prominence of the research enterprise, we should begin asking how its potential to enrich undergraduate liberal education could be more fully realized. Critics have long argued that the reward structure of the academy should change so that incentives for teaching equal those for research. This outcome is unlikely, however. The problem is more apt to be overcome by reconceiving research in ways that make it more teachable.[15]

Again, the point should be to exploit the untapped potential of existing practices before we assume that something totally different is necessary. Before writing off the present research system, we should give it a fair chance by seeing how well it functioned if its components for once worked together.

Such a step would amount to giving students a fairer chance as well. Before getting carried away by alarms about all the classics students allegedly have not read and all the facts they allegedly do not know, we should ask how reasonable our expectations of students' prowess have been when we consider the conditions of their exposure to academic culture. We would not be surprised if our hypothetical novice who was introduced to baseball in the disjunctive, position-by-position way I imagined above were to score poorly on a baseball cultural literacy quiz, not knowing the significance of names like Bobby Bonilla and Rickey Henderson or terms like "split-finger fastball." Yet we would be foolish to blame this failure on the novice, much less on major-league baseball for having specializations such as shortstops, designated hitters, and pitching coaches. Before we blamed someone's failure to comprehend a game on either the person or the game, we would look at the conditions under which the learning of the game was taking place. We would try to assess what might be called the intelligibility conditions of the activity, the conditions under which it figures to become intelligible to people not already familiar with it.

Bloom fails to stay with the best part of his own analysis long enough to arrive at this point. But, then, this fruitful part of his analysis, his critique of curricular disjunction, would not support the kind of moral indignation that can be whipped up by denunciations of students, teachers, and specialized research. So Bloom is left with a dramatic but finally vacuous plea for what he calls "the good old great books tradition," in which, presumably, "university-wide agreement" would be embodied. How this agreement is to be achieved he does not say. We need a more constructive analysis than this of the roots of curricular incoherence, and I will try to provide one in the next chapter with a further look at educational history.

Chapter 7

Burying the Battlefield, or, a Short History of How the Curriculum Became a Cafeteria Counter

IF history, as it has been said, is a story in which the winners bury the losers, the modern curriculum could be said to be a story in which the battlefield itself is buried.[1] The history of higher education is a succession of stormy conflicts that have produced the curriculum but are rarely addressed in it. What I would like to show in this chapter is the role played by the concealment of these conflicts in producing the cafeteria counter curriculum whose incoherence so many critics now deplore. My analysis is an alternative to the view that blames the cafeteria counter curriculum and its deficiencies on the shattering of a traditional consensus by political pressures from special interest groups.

Let's Make a Deal

ONCE upon a time, according to this nostalgic view, subjects entered the curriculum the old-fashioned way: They earned it. Then, in the late 1960s, "politics" suddenly intruded, and it has been all downhill since then. Former Secretary Bennett, for example, states that it was "during the late 1960s and early 1970s" that "a collective loss of nerve and faith . . . was undeniably destructive of the curriculum." In this narrative the sixties become the fatal turning point, after which, as Bennett puts it, "the curriculum was no longer a statement about what knowledge mattered; instead it became a political compromise among competing schools and departments overlaid by marketing considerations."[2]

Bennett's fellow conservative Diane Ravitch, however, says that the politics of clashing interest groups has produced disagreements over "what knowledge mattered" since the beginnings of mass education around the turn of the century and that political pressures have always played a major role in the resolution of these disagreements. Of course, a good deal depends on how words like "politics" and "political" are used, and the looseness with which they have been tossed about in the current dispute seems to me to have worked to the advantage of conservatives like Bennett. (I leave these problems of definition to my next chapter, however.) As Ravitch points out with respect to the schools—and her point is applicable to the colleges as well—"questions of race, ethnicity, and religion have been a perennial source of conflict in American education. . . . In our history, the schools have been not only an institution in which to teach young people skills and knowledge but an arena where interest groups fight to preserve their values, or to revise the judgments of history, or to bring about fundamental social change." At the same time, Ravitch adds, "such divisive questions were usually excluded from the curriculum. The textbooks minimized the problems among groups and taught a sanitized version of history" in which conflicts were effaced or minimized.[3]

The complaint that "marketing considerations" have undermined the common culture, causing the curriculum no longer to be "a statement about what knowledge mattered," was already a commonplace of American educational critics as early as the first decade of the twentieth century. In 1907, for example, one professor noted that "popular 'snap' courses for miscellaneous good-natured auditors"[4] seemed to be springing up everyplace and that "for all but a small minority of ambitious undergraduates, incoherence in the choice of courses and the mechanical accumulation of course-credits" had become "the order of the day." Another observer in 1912 complained that the university had "caught the spirit of the business world, its desire for great things—large enrollments, great equipment, puffed advertisement, sensational features, strenuous competition, underbidding."[5] In 1908 an English scholar complained to his colleagues at the annual meeting of the Modern Language Association of "the sacrifice of the student's good to the pleasure of the instructor," who "offers the course in which he has specialized, or in which he wishes to carry on special study." As a result, this scholar observed, literary study had been broken up into so great a "number of subdivisions" that a student "may take one or even two such subjects thru [sic] several terms of his course, and get no connected idea of the literature in his mother tongue."[6]

Another professor, looking back on his teaching stint in the Harvard English department in the same period, wrote as follows, in terms that will be familiar to anyone who has been keeping up with today's jeremiads against the loss of a common culture:

> It was difficult for a stranger to discover any common denominator of their activities. What was the underlying philosophy of the department, its ideal aim, its relation to liberal studies as a whole? . . . Fundamental questions were avoided at our meetings; the precious time was consumed in the discussion of wearisome administrative details. The separate parts of the English machine seemed to be in competent hands, but how were the parts related?[7]

Such statements (and many more like them could be furnished) make it clear that the perception was already widespread by the early twentieth century that the curriculum had no "common denominator," that it was, as we say today, a mere cafeteria counter of professorial research interests. Then, as now, the complaint went hand in hand with the assumption that without a common denominator no way exists to connect the "separate parts" of the academic machine, that a common discussion is possible only if there is bedrock consensus.

This was a self-defeating assumption from the outset, if only because the distinctive feature of the modern American university was its proliferation of differences. Such differences had been kept out of the small liberal arts colleges that constituted the system of American higher education from the seventeenth century down to the Civil War. These colleges were dominated by a strict ideological and social orthodoxy resting on the twin pillars of the Christian religion and the Greek and Latin languages. Latent conflicts that might have threatened the unity of the college were forestalled by the simple tactic of excluding anyone who seriously dissented from these articles of faith. The complaint that the curriculum has been taken over by marketing considerations and political compromises inevitably expresses a certain nostalgia for the lost unity of the old college, though most conservatives today would probably regard such a return as unthinkable.

The predemocratic college curriculum had been strictly unified around a small number of basic subjects, the central ones being Greek and Latin, Christian theology, and moral philosophy. Those who went through the experience left ample testimony that it was usually a deadly grind. This was due not only to the restricted number of subjects but also to the severely regimented way they were taught; Greek and Latin classes, for example, involved formal recitations that concentrated on grammatical and etymological points and ignored the broader meanings of the literature. The rationale for this method lay in the prevailing philosophy of "mental discipline," which held that in order to strengthen the student's character, academic study should involve punishing, routine drill work. The assumption seems also to have been that any gentleman of good breeding would naturally intuit the *meaning* of a literary work and therefore had no need to descend to interpreting the sorts of hidden meanings that became the staple of literature courses as this gentlemanly assumption waned.

The classical curriculum came under mounting attack throughout the nineteenth century for its irrelevance to the kinds of lives most younger Americans could look forward to, but the leading colleges fought successfully until the end of the century to keep it unchanged. Led by Yale, the chief bastion of tradition, college presidents took pride in the fact that their institutions represented only a tiny elite, enrolling less than 2 percent of the eligible population and functioning as training schools for the ministry and a few other professions like medicine and law. Colleges also functioned as social finishing schools for young men of the genteel class (and for women after the establishment of women's colleges around mid-century) and for a scattering of others who hoped to rise into that class. Colleges saw themselves as small beacons of civilization in a society otherwise given over to crass materialism; to serve the needs of popular democracy would have been to sell their souls.

All this changed when the old college gave way to the modern research university, powered by the scientific ideal of knowledge production and the vocational ideal of preparation for careers in business, industry, and agriculture. The old fixed curriculum, which had obliged students for the most part to study a common set of subjects, gave way to the elective system, pioneered by Harvard's president Charles William Eliot and established at most campuses by the turn of the century, allowing students a range of course options that in some instances was almost as wide as it is today. In this expansion of educational interests and functions, the traditional dedication to liberal learning (then called "liberal culture") was coupled with the modern enterprises of research and vocationalism. Higher education was suddenly no longer culturally and intellectually monolithic, and the problem of conflict resolution presented itself. Though university education was still largely for the elite classes, it needed a means of reconciling a mixture of components that was far more diverse and potentially divisive than anything yet experienced anywhere in higher education.

In one of its phases the conflict took the form of a quarrel between "pure" research and knowledge aimed at practical vocational applications. But a deeper quarrel pitted research scholars as such, whether pure or applied, against those who still defended a less rigorous, more moralistic and traditional view of liberal culture, which became increasingly identified with what later was called the humanities. The humanities themselves became a scene of this conflict since they were defended as both a rival of science and a branch of science.

Two Kinds of Humanists

ON the one hand, humanities departments still saw themselves as an instrument for the old college mission of preserving and transmitting the traditional cultural heritage of the literary and philosophical classics, "classics" that were now English and European rather than Greek and Latin. Though the modern humanities claimed descent from the humanists of the Renaissance who had recovered ancient classical learning, the "humanism" that influenced them most deeply and directly was the Victorian idealism of men of letters like Matthew Arnold and John Ruskin. On the other hand, in order to gain respect as a "department" in the modern research university, academic humanists had to establish themselves as scientific investigators, bringing the same rigor to the study of languages and literatures that physicists and chemists brought to the study of nature. Humanities departments based their scientific credentials on the philological study of languages and culture that enterprising

American scholars had been bringing back from German graduate schools since the early nineteenth century.

In theory there was no conflict between these conceptions of the humanities, and this belief in an essential harmony between preserving tradition and acquiring new knowledge has always been the official claim of the university. From 1900 to 1990 the rhetoric of college catalogs, presidential oratory, and fundraising and recruitment propaganda has stressed that the college or university is firmly committed to both the preservation of the old and the encouragement of the new. In fact, however, the old and the new clashed, resulting in a dramatic split between two kinds of academic humanists, the research professional dedicated to the production of new knowledge for an audience of other professionals and the generalist man of letters dedicated to teaching rather than research and to promoting the spirit of the humanities among the public at large.

In the early language and literature departments, research scholars concentrated on minutely specialized linguistic investigations, published in formidable professional journals like the *Publications of the Modern Language Association,* that were comprehensible to few besides other specialists. Their careers were tied to a professional field network which regulated the academic marketplace of positions. Though some had broader literary interests of an aesthetic or a philosophical kind, these interests played hardly any role in their work, and there were early philologists like Kemp Malone of Johns Hopkins who actually opposed the English department's becoming involved with literature on the ground that this would corrupt philology with belletrism.

As for the men of letters (most of whom were indeed male), these were public intellectuals who disdained the professional network and its academic journals and wrote appreciative essays for general-circulation magazines like the *Atlantic Monthly* and the *Nation,* where they sometimes held editorial positions between teaching stints. Like their scholarly colleagues, the men of letters thought of literary study as a "profession," but in a journalistic way that harked back to eighteenth-century generalists such as Joseph Addison, Richard Steele, and Samuel Johnson. These early academic generalists, like John Erskine of Columbia University (a pioneer of great books courses), William Lyon Phelps of Yale, and Bliss Perry of Harvard and Princeton, exemplified what they called the "amateur spirit." Literature for them was about spiritual and social values, not the pedantic etymologies, linguistic laws, and antiquarian facts that seemed to be the only thing the research scholars could find in it.

Even before the turn of the century it was widely noted that a deep and unhealthy gulf separated the amateur man of letters and the research professional, the one tending in his publishing and teaching to be provocative but impressionistic, the other tending to be rigorous but dull. In this early rift we can see the seeds of the later conflict between the academic knowledge industry and literary journalism.

And yet—in view of the violence that marks this conflict of academics and journalists today—what seems remarkable in retrospect about the earlier phase of the conflict is how few reverberations it had inside or outside the university. Part of this was owing to the fact that deep, unspoken social bonds united the early research scholars and men of letters, making them allies against what they saw as a philistine American public that unashamedly cared about neither research nor polite letters. Even so, the differences between the groups were deep and acrimonious enough to have been disruptive, yet these differences hardly ruffled the placid atmosphere of the university or impeded the steady growth of the humanities. Why was this?

Laurence R. Veysey provides a convincing answer in his standard work *The Emergence of the American University*. When the new university replaced the old college, Veysey observes, bureaucratic administration to a large extent replaced a commonly shared philosophy as the cement that held the university together. Neither Christianity nor science nor literary humanism proved capable of synthesizing the full range of knowledge and opinion now encompassed by the university. The university "was fast becoming an institution beholden to no metaphysic," and "talk about the higher purposes of the university" was "increasingly ritualistic."[8] Instead, the university learned to operate "without recourse to specific shared values," and what made this possible was the structural device of bureaucratic administration.[9]

But Veysey points out that the new bureaucratic structure discouraged not only "specific shared values" but also the airing of disagreements. Disagreement was thought to be an embarrassment by old traditionalists and new professionals alike since it threatened the unity of the cultural tradition on the one hand and the steady progress of knowledge on the other. "Quarrelsome debate," Veysey writes, "including that based upon conflicts among academic ideals," had to "be minimized or suppressed whenever it became threateningly serious."[10] He describes the new academic structure as one of "patterned isolation," in which "each academic group normally refrained from too rude or brutal an unmasking of the rest. . . . The university throve, as it were, on ignorance."[11]

In at least one key respect, then, the more things changed, the more they stayed the same. Whereas the old college had avoided controversy by excluding dissenters, the new university avoided it by keeping dissenters apart. Whereas the old college had blindly resisted innovation, the new university painlessly absorbed the most threatening novelties by the simple device of adding new components to an ever-expanding aggregate. A former English department chair, Gary Waller, has called this additive device "the park-bench principle of curricular change. When a powerful newcomer shows up, everyone on the bench shuffles over just a little to make room for the latest arrival. Occasionally, if things get a little crowded, the one at the end falls off—Anglo-Saxon, perhaps, or philology."[12]

The structure of patterned isolation defused academic con-

flicts by keeping warring factions in noncommunicating departments, fields, and courses, areas that were now to be "covered"
by teachers and students. Soon each subject had its own rooms,
buildings, or sector of the campus—the history department in
the old Gothic building on the hill, the social sciences in functional quarters near the administration building, the natural sciences in newer but always crammed laboratory towers, and later
the business school in a plush modern office complex with rooms
named for corporate donors. It was now possible for professors
to spend whole careers without ever encountering some of their
colleagues even in allied departments.

In other words, potential conflicts like the one that divided
old-fashioned humanists and newfangled research professionals
were avoided by precisely the sort of political trade-offs for which
the 1960s have lately been made the scapegoat. The new form
of academic organization enforced an undeclared truce among
potentially clashing fields and values by keeping them in separate courses, departmental buildings, and faculty offices. As long
as scientists and humanists, antiquarians and modernists, specialists and generalists covered their assigned portions of the
departmental and curricular turf, there was no need to debate
their often antithetical aims and methods.

Contrary to Secretary Bennett, then, it was closer to 1900
than to 1965 that the curriculum ceased to be based on a consensus "about what knowledge mattered" and became "a political compromise among competing schools and departments
overlaid by marketing considerations." Of course, the specifically ideological dimension of these conflicts has come more
nakedly to the fore as the social homogeneity of the campus has
eroded and as the politics of a gentlemanly consensus has given
way to the more polarized politics of left and right. But for almost
a century now the curriculum has been not a unified statement
about what knowledge mattered but a collection of disconnected and often antagonistic fields, adding up to neither a con-

sensus nor a set of active disagreements and held together by political bargaining.

And for almost a century now critics have been complaining about this state of affairs in ritualistic and ineffectual ways. The myth of an educational past free of politics and marketing considerations, which presumably can be restored if we will only throw certain troublemakers out, appeals powerfully to our frustration at a long history of educational failures. Invoking the myth is an effective means of stirring up popular indignation against academic factions one disagrees with. The price that we pay for falsifying history, however, is that we learn nothing from our past mistakes.

Taking Cover in Coverage

A COLLEGE organized around a philosophical and social consensus had given way to a modern university organized around the coverage of separate professional research fields. This "field coverage model" (as I shall be calling it here) reconciled or papered over the unresolved contradictions between tradition and professionalism on which the modern university had been founded. And despite periodic flare-ups of discontent, it did so in a fashion that left all sides relatively satisfied for a long time. As long as conflicting individuals and factions had little to do with each other, it was still possible to maintain the illusion that a common cultural tradition was intact.[13]

The field coverage model satisfied the research professionals, for it organized the department in accordance with the most up-to-date and efficient principles of bureaucratic management. A department fully staffed, covering the major periods, topics, and subfields, was well primed for the research productivity that would attract promising graduate students and earn it a reputation in the international world of the disciplines. Yet the field coverage principle managed to satisfy most traditional humanists as well. If one assumed that teachers and students covered a reasonable spread of standard periods, the experience would presumably add up in students' minds to a sense of the common culture.

This was a polite fiction, for if the field coverage model preserved the semblance of stable commonality, its real effect was to stimulate innovation and diversity. By simply adding new fields to an expanding aggregate, the university could increase the range of subjects, cultures, and literatures to be studied and could incorporate new approaches without risking the major collisions and turf wars that would otherwise have occurred. The university could welcome innovation without the onerous need to redraw the curricular and disciplinary map every time it did so, and it could keep traditionalist discontents over innovation at bay. The literary canon could be continuously revised to make it more diverse and up-to-date without losing at least the appearance— though again it was never much more than that—of a unified literary tradition. By the 1960s this openness to revision had resulted in a far more culturally representative academic culture than had existed in the past (and, for that reason, a more candid acknowledgment by some of the place of politics in the academy), and the field coverage principle deserved much of the credit.

But these gains came at a high price. Insofar as controversy is the life and soul of a democratic intellectual institution, the consequences of avoiding or muffling it—or of making it the province of the extracurricular life of the college—could only be harmful to the curriculum, which was left without a means of connecting subjects, perspectives, and courses and thus of confronting its own most urgent disagreements. Instead of becoming centers of continuous intellectual discussion, universities quarantined the intellectual life within the hours of class time, creating a deep disjunction between the intellectual intensity of the classroom and the social life of the campus. It was not the existence of bureaucratic fields in themselves that was the problem, or even the idea that these fields should be "covered," but the failure to develop a principle of connection that would have opened a dialogue among them.

One of the advantages of the field coverage principle of organization was that it made departments and curricula virtually self-administering. Once the conventional spread of fields was fully staffed and the courses were accordingly distributed and assigned, larger questions about the aims of the humanities and sciences and the relations of disparate periods, methodologies, and values seemingly took care of themselves. Such questions might come up in a course here and there, but there was no need to debate them collectively, and no arena for doing so. In a sense, the field coverage principle solved the problem of "theory," by making it unnecessary to have a theory of the university or a debate among conflicting theories. Not that theoretical choices had not been made, but they seemed to have been taken care of by the grid of periods, genres, and other catalog rubrics, which in the aggregate bespoke a seemingly confident and uncontroversial statement of what the department and the university were all about.

The other great advantage of the field coverage principle, its receptivity to innovation, enabled threatening new ideas and forms of culture to be overlaid on traditional approaches and literatures without the need to confront the resulting conflicts of ideology, much less make them an issue for students to be aware of. Novel theories and practices that challenged traditional ones could be accepted and given their own courses or programs where they would no longer be a bother. When a threatening innovation appeared—modernist literature, the New Criticism, avant-garde art, Marxist economics, creative writing, econometrics, psychohistory, feminism, or deconstruction—its proponents, after an initial period of struggle, could be appeased by the addition of a new course, program, or department to the aggregate. But the traditionalists who opposed the innovation were also appeased since they did not have to alter their own practices or engage in serious debate with the newcomers. Thus the new professional conditions, though open to innovation in a way the old college had never been, discouraged attempts to assess the meaning of an innovation or its compatibility or incompatibility with traditional practices.

In this way explosive contradictions proliferated in the academy without being felt *as* contradictions, since their separation in different courses, departments, and campus buildings prevented teachers and students from experiencing them as such. It came to seem perfectly normal that philosophies in deadly rivalry with one another should be taught in adjacent rooms at the same hour, with no attempt to take stock of the rivalry except what students might be able to manage on their own. As in a museum where the tourist can stroll from neoclassicism to pop art, postimpressionism, and dada without experiencing any sense of discrepancy, it seemed normal for students to move between violently clashing courses without being asked to consider the meaning of the clash or even to notice its existence. It is this ability to efface or normalize contradictions that explains how, as I noted earlier, the university can have become a staging ground of subversive cultural experimentation without losing its reputation as an official guardian of tradition and how traditionalists and revisionists can each with some justice believe the opposing party is in control.

The separation of undergraduate general education from specialized graduate training was another expression of the tacit political bargain between teachers and researchers. It was mutually understood that the research specialists would control the graduate seminar, while the generalists would hold sway in the large freshman and sophomore introductory courses and win the college teaching awards. In the no-man's-land between graduate study and general education was the departmental major, whose content became a constant tug-of-war between those who would make it a preprofessional program for future graduate students and those who would infuse it with the values of the cultivated amateur. The major could have been enriched by the acknowledgment of this conflict, but like the other conflicts of the department, this one was fought out behind the scenes, in faculty meetings that students did not attend or in the pages of specialized journals that students did not read.

Not that what was debated at faculty meetings or in professional journals would have always been interesting or edifying to students. But buried in the departmental turf wars and the technical language of the journals was a set of conflicts that were far from trivial, conflicts about the very nature of knowledge and its place in modern society: Was the most important knowledge scientific or humanistic, or in some measure both? What did these terms mean, and what was their relation? Was the increasing professionalization of knowledge good or bad? How should one sort out the often sharply conflicting claims of the pre- and post-1800 worlds, both of which students were in some measure expected to cover? What about the social functions of science, art, and criticism, about which debate increasingly raged? What was the place, if there was a place, of high culture in America, and what was its relation to the popular media?

The university *contained* a host of conflicting answers to these large questions, but it did not engage them. And this evasion of conflict, which structured the relations of the faculty and its courses, was reproduced in the curriculum and passed on to students. Students covered a sampling of research fields without being expected to be aware of the struggles and alliances which underlay and to a large extent defined the field divisions. Thus arose the kind of experience we looked at in the last chapter, in which a student senses an antagonism between, say, a literature and a sociology course but is not let in on the sources of the antagonism and what it may mean.

So the curriculum evolved as a curious archaeological overlay, a result of conflicts that have been forgotten without leaving a trace. Take the conflict between the sciences and the humanities. Since neither the science nor the humanities faculty is responsible for dealing with this conflict (and since neither is capable of dealing with it without the collaboration of the other), the conflict falls into the cracks between the sciences and the humanities. Students are required to cover a certain number of sciences and humanities, but it is left up to them to think about the relation of the two, even though it is hard to understand the historical emergence and significance of either without the other.

The same was true of the conflicts and convergences between literature and the visual arts and, more recently, between literature and creative writing and literature and composition; and between philosophy, history, the social sciences, psychology, anthropology, economics, mathematics, history of science, rhetoric and communications, and studio art and art history. Since these conflicts between departments and courses were not the responsibility of any department or course, they rarely became central in courses until recent interdisciplinary programs, such as American studies or women's studies, began addressing them. These interdisciplinary programs have been valuable, but since they are usually themselves incorporated as yet another add-on, they tend to become one more fragment on the margin rather than a means of connecting the fragments, reproducing the fragmentation they set out to cure. Thus the relation between disciplinary and interdisciplinary study has become another submerged conflict rather than a means of giving focus to the curriculum.

Critics have often commented on the inexorable way the divisions of the curriculum come to seem natural and inevitable, as if they are simply beyond human control. Once the standard historical periods were intact for a generation or so, the Renaissance and the eighteenth century did come to seem like unalterable facts of nature even though everyone knows they are human conceptual contrivances whose validity is controversial. As the literary theorist Robert Scholes observes, "we often assume that the development of a curriculum is an innocent occupation, for which we need accept no personal responsibility. The 'masterpieces' are *there* and so we teach them. They have been pre-selected by culture, laid down like fossils in the sedimented layers of institutional tradition. Our only duty is to make them relevant."[14] The isolation of these subjects in noncommunicating courses contributes to their unreflective appearance of *thereness* since it prevents the sort of regular debate that could force us to be more reflective about how the subjects got there in the first place. Students are thus asked to study the canon without concern for the complex processes of judgment, debate, and struggle by which it became canonical.

Where Do We Go from Here?

THE ideological polarizations of the university have continued to deepen, but in the absence of any structural need to confront them they still can often be ignored, except when hiring and tenure decisions or curricular reform proposals rudely force them into view. At such moments long-repressed conflicts erupt in open rage, with their aftermath of backbiting and hatred. The ensuing failure to debate conflicts productively then tends to be blamed on innate aspects of the professorial temperament rather than on institutional arrangements which might be changed. Increasingly shell-shocked by the sense of a permanent state of war, many teachers and administrators harbor no loftier hope than somehow to maintain a nervous peace and quiet.

But keeping philosophical differences among the faculty from erupting into open dispute is increasingly difficult. New fields like women's studies, ethnic studies, and the various forms of theory, which had seemed safely ghettoized, appear ever more to be encroaching on the space once dominated by traditional thinking. The playing field turns out not to be infinite after all, and a shrinking economy further constrains it, making it harder to resolve conflicts in the old painless way by appeasing all parties. That a concerted attack on women's and ethnic studies programs is only now being mounted after these programs have been in existence for some thirty years suggests that what is really found threatening is that these programs have achieved a measure of power.

It is understandable that the targeted programs tend to react to the attack on them by adopting a bunker mentality and seeking to protect their hard-won turf from further erosion.But though this may be a necessary strategy in the short run, it seems to me both tactically and educationally unwise in the long run. The bunker mentality leads to self-marginalization rather than to the open and democratic debate that iconoclastic minorities need in order to bring their ideas to a wider public, clarify them for students, and protect them from misrepresentations. This is why I suggested in Chapter 1 that it is a mistake to institutionalize "cultural diversity" as a set of separate course requirements, as numerous campuses today are attempting to do. If the very idea of cultural diversity implies dialogue and debate rather than isolation and marginalization, then non-Western culture needs to be put into dialogue with Western culture, if only to see how much meaning these terms have. Simply asking students to cover a certain number of units of each is an evasion of such dialogue. While in one way it constitutes an innovation, in a deeper way it replicates one of the most deadening aspects of educational tradition.

Conservatives are right, then, to argue that today's curriculum is the result of political bargaining and trade-offs rather than a commonly shared educational philosophy. But what conservatives deplore has been the state of the curriculum for almost a century now. The curriculum was not free from politics until the sixties, only then to be suddenly overtaken by them. Rather, as the curriculum has been democratized, its political rivalries have become more dramatic and openly political.

Instead of blaming the incoherence of the curriculum on politics—as if this were not itself a political tactic—we would behave more productively if we were to try to exploit the conflicts of principle that underlie our political conflicts and tap their unused educational potential. For contrary to the assumption that has dominated the recent debate, politics need not be a corrupting intrusion into the purity of principled educational thought. Political conflict at its best is fought out as a battle of ideas, arguments, and principles.

It is when the principles underlying institutional politics are buried from public view that those politics tend to become unedifying, since differences then express themselves in rancor, calumny, and insult rather than in principled argument. Instead of endlessly lamenting the intrusion of politics into the curriculum, we would do better to bring into the curriculum itself whatever may be instructive in the clashes of political and philosophical principles that have shaped it. The lament itself bespeaks a poverty of imagination, unable as it is to imagine how conflict, disagreement, and difference might themselves become a source of educational and cultural coherence—indeed, the appropriate source of coherence for a democratic society.

Chapter 8

When Is Something "Political"?

GEORGE ORWELL once wrote that "no book is genuinely free from political bias. The opinion that art should have nothing to do with politics is itself a political attitude."[1] Orwell was by no means the only respected writer of his generation to hold that art is unavoidably political. The belief was embraced by Edmund Wilson, Georg Lukács, Bertolt Brecht, Jean Paul Sartre, Walter Benjamin, and Van Wyck Brooks, among others. Nor was the belief restricted to the far left. Conservatives like T. S. Eliot and liberals like Thomas Mann agreed with socialists like Orwell that the arts profoundly reflect and influence the political shape of society. One of the most influential books on American literature ever written—F. O. Matthiessen's *American Renaissance,* published in 1941—located the "common denominator" of the major nineteenth-century American writers in a political attitude, "their devotion to the possibilities of democracy."[2] Alfred Kazin, in his almost equally influential *On Native Grounds* (1942), wrote that criticism in America had always been "predominantly social, even political, in its thinking," more "a form of moral propaganda than a study in aesthetic problems." From Emerson and Thoreau to Mencken and Brooks, Kazin wrote, "criticism had been the great American lay philosophy, the intellectual conscience and intellectual carryall. It had been a study of literature inherently concerned with ideals of citizenship, and often less a study of literary texts than a search for some new and imperative moral order within which American writing could live and grow."[3]

The view that art cannot be sharply separated from "politics"—defined broadly as a concern with the welfare of the polity and the relations of social groups—has occupied an honored place among the numerous theories of art—moral, religious, formal, psychological—that have competed for preeminence throughout the history of criticism. Plato became the first great political critic when he expelled the poets from his republic for threatening the moral stability of the state. From Aristotle to Sir Philip Sidney, John Milton, and Samuel Johnson, major critics answered Plato by turning his argument around and crediting poetry with salutary political effects, while romantics like William Blake and Percy Shelley went even further, asserting that poetry is society's ultimate weapon against tyranny.

The Denial of Politics

TODAY, however, a strenuous effort is being made to pretend that this history never existed. The philosopher John Searle flatly asserts that "in the study of most great works of literature, the political dimension is minor. You will miss the point of, say, Proust or Shakespeare if you think that their main interest is the bearing of their work on the sort of political preoccupations that we happen to have today."[4] So much for Blake, Wilson, and Orwell, not to mention traditional scholarship on Shakespeare's persistent concern with questions of royal authority and usurpation and Proust's critique of bourgeois decadence or his ambivalent view of homosexuality.

One might think that Searle, as an analytic philosopher and

thus professionally concerned with disentangling confusions over words, would pause over the fact that the word "politics" is used in very different senses by today's politically oriented academic critics and their detractors. As understood by the editors of a recent collection entitled *Political Shakespeare,* for example, recent political criticism of Shakespeare concerns itself not with the narrow "sort of political preoccupations that we happen to have today," as Searle calls them, but with "the whole system of significations by which a society or a section of it understands itself and its relations with the world."[5] There can be little real debate over the politics of culture as long as one party defines the "political" so comprehensively while the other defines it as a narrow instrument of propaganda.

The problem, however, is pedagogical as well as theoretical. The concern of critics like Searle is that teachers today, in his phrase, are "using the classroom to impose a specific ideology on students."[6] This concern seems to me legitimate enough. The passionate hostilities unleashed by the culture war do indeed pose serious questions about the proper limits of politics in our classrooms. Of all the academic constituencies, students are the most vulnerable to ideological coercion. Whereas administrators are cushioned by their distance from the day-to-day business of teaching and learning, and professors are cushioned by the privacy of their classrooms, students occupy an exposed position in the middle of the battlefield. There is something unhealthy about a roomful of students who feel under pressure to accede to the professor's politics, whether the tilt is to the left, right, or center. And there is something unhealthy about teachers who endlessly preach to the converted, never having to encounter an opposing view from anyone of equal authority.

The problems posed by "politicized" teaching need to be examined with more judiciousness, however, than has been shown by Searle and other angry critics, who treat such words as a club rather than a concept to be analyzed. Such critics are too quick to assume that intolerance, rigidity, and closed-mindedness automatically follow when teachers take stances on political issues.

Because he operates on this assumption, Searle can offer only a draconian prescription to the teacher: "[W]here possible the professor should leave his or her political views out of the classroom."[7] Searle grants that this is not possible in some fields, like political theory and the history of the Russian Revolution. But in these cases, he says, "the professor should simply state his or her own political commitments at the beginning and then in the course of the term make sure that he or she presents the strongest possible arguments for all relevant views, including those that differ from his or her own."[8]

This seems eminently sensible, but it ignores the fact that "political commitments" are often expressed in the very choice of what to include or not include in a course. Recently I have been corresponding with a well-known conservative sociologist who insists he so scrupulously avoids betraying any hint of his politics in his teaching that many of his students cannot tell what they are. After taking his seminar on Marxism, he says, several students complained that he had not revealed his own views on Marxism, a reproach he took as an unintended compliment. "It so happens," he writes, "that my views of Marxism were no more ambiguous than they are now, but this was not a course about my views." In the mere act of teaching Marxism at all, however, my correspondent conveyed his "view" that Marxism is a respectable body of thought or at least one that merits study. This may seem trivial, hardly a "political commitment" at all, but it would not have seemed so to a political scientist I once encountered in a lecture audience, who asked me why I had included Marxism in a list of presumably legitimate philosophies, something he likened to including the flat earth theory in a survey of contemporary astronomy.

In my own teaching I think of myself as concerned more with clarifying debates over politics than with pushing a particular commitment, but I suspect that colleagues to the left of me would find my teaching too conservative and those to the right of me too radical. When I delivered a talk to the National Association of Scholars based on the account in Chapter 2 of how I teach the debate over politics on *Heart of Darkness,* several members of that conservative organization praised me during the discussion period for my intelligent solution to the controversy. But when a version of the talk was later published in the *Chronicle,* I was attacked in several letters to the editor for "political correctness."[9] How "political" you are as a teacher is partly in the eye of the beholder, and it varies with the context.

Searle has a valid goal: to prevent the corruption of intellectual inquiry and teaching by ideological true believers. But his proscription of politics would toss out the social commitment that often gives passion to teaching along with the bath water of ideological dogmatism. Searle's view of politics as something to be gotten out of the way as soon as possible in order to get on with the real business of teaching seems to me another example of the essentially frightened and defensive way of thinking about conflict that characterizes so much recent educational criticism. The assumption is that political conflict is a kind of disease that must somehow be contained, if it cannot be entirely avoided, instead of a potential source of intellectual and cultural vitality to be tapped. This refusal to confront political conflicts head-on only makes them more poisonous when they do surface.

Since Searle regards every form of classroom politicization as evil, he cannot discriminate between legitimate and illegitimate versions of it. Clearly he does not intend it, but by his criteria, a professor who attacked the evils of South African apartheid would be as guilty of politicizing his classroom as one who failed students for refusing to agree with Marx or Edmund Burke. The problem is that Searle makes no distinction between (1) raising political questions in a classroom, (2) endorsing a particular answer to those questions in a way that leaves the discussion open for disagreement, and (3) "using the classroom to impose a specific ideology on students." By condemning "politicization" as such, this view obscures the crucial distinction between *expressing* a political view in a class and *imposing* it forcibly on students and colleagues.

Such conflation would obviously leave us helpless to deal with political conflict when it arises in teaching situations, as it always has in the past and is all the more likely to in today's highly charged climate. To deal usefully with the question of politics and the classroom, I suggest we must be willing to consider certain questions open rather than closed: How far is it actually possible for a teacher to "leave his or her political views out of the classroom"? Do not political views get conveyed in indirect ways, starting with the very choice of what is to be studied and not studied? Where do political judgments end and intellectual and aesthetic judgments begin, and can a clear line be drawn between them? In short, what do we mean by being "political" in teaching or in general?

History Once More

AS with so many other issues in the culture war, discussion of the politics of teaching takes place under the shadow of a mythical academic past, in this case a past from which the politics have been conveniently erased. Here is Joseph Epstein in *Commentary* describing how the politically minded English teacher was once supposedly dealt with:

> In the old days, one can imagine a strong English-department chairman, in the approved English-professor manner, taking Prof. X aside to say, "Look here, X, do be a good fellow and forget that rot about the bourgeois attitudes of the New England writers I understand you are teaching. Publish it if you like—that is your business. But our business, as teachers, is sticking to the text." If professor X were tenured, the request would be a friendly one; if he were not yet tenured, the request would no doubt be more insistent.

Today, Epstein says, "our chairman would be accused, at a minimum, of McCarthyism, fascism, and troglodyticism. . . . But not to worry, no chairman is likely to suggest that Prof. X knock it off. It just isn't done."[10]

In a way Epstein is right. The obnoxious little scene he constructs *does* indicate the way academic departments often handled politics "in the old days." What is troubling is that such paternalistic bullying should be Epstein's idea of the *right* way to run a university. Evidently it is not important that young Professor X actually believes the "rot" he is teaching "about the bourgeois attitudes of the New England writers" or that in analyzing those attitudes he thinks he *is* "sticking to the text," since those bourgeois attitudes are presumably in the text. Nor is he likely to understand how it can be all right for him to publish his ideas if he likes but not to teach them. It does not seem to occur to Epstein that a world in which a code of academic freedom restrains authorities from telling you to "knock off" teaching what you believe is an improvement over a world in which it did not.

In the actual old days, of course, few department chairs had to contend with heterodox views about the "bourgeois attitudes of New England writers" since professors who entertained such views were not encouraged to apply. Most Marxist criticism in the 1930s was written by journalists, not academics, and the few Marxists who did become academics were not invited to "publish it if you like" or warned to "knock it off." They were discontinued or fired, like Granville Hicks, who was the nation's leading Marxist critic when he was let go in 1935 by Rensselaer Polytechnic Institute.[11]

The fact is that in the American university a heavy concentration of radicals in a field tends to stand out because it is so unusual. Throughout most of the modern history of the university, patriotic nationalism has been so taken for granted as the *natural* background of academic culture that it has not been seen as a form of politics at all. In literature and the humanities, cultural nationalism has been the main organizing principle since the romantic period, when the doctrine became established that the quality of a nation's language and literature was the touchstone of its greatness as a nation. Possession of a great literature enabled nations to justify imperial ambitions abroad and demands on the loyalty of citizens at home.

The ideology that propelled the growth of English as an academic discipline was a kind of literary mixture of the doctrines of manifest destiny and social Darwinism: Since the culture of the English-speaking races is in the ascendant, it must be superior to other cultures and therefore deserves to be spread. As an American professor and textbook writer put it in 1896, a nation's "literature is likely to be strong and great in proportion as the peoples who speak the language are strong and great." He added that "English literature is therefore likely to grow, as it is the record of the life of the English speaking race and as this race is steadily spreading abroad over the globe."[12] Clearly the professor was giving vent to what we now would recognize as political propaganda, yet it is not recorded that his department chair took him aside and said, "Publish it if you like, but forget that rot about the English-speaking race."

By the "English speaking race" the professor meant the Anglo-Saxon racial stock, the purest manifestations of which were supposedly distilled in the English literary classics. It was because it embodied this pure Anglo-Saxon spirit that English literature was thought to possess great educational value as a means of socializing increasingly heterogeneous masses of students, many of them newly arrived immigrants, into the culture of their betters. The dissemination of the Anglo-Saxon spirit was what one of the British pioneers of English studies had in mind when in 1891 he made a plea for English studies as an "instrument of political education."[13] A later educational report writer made even clearer the element of social control that animated the development of English studies, arguing that English would create "a national fellowship in which it shall be possible for everyone to forget the existence of classes."[14]

When the controversy erupted after the Civil War over the proposal that English literature take over the central position in the American curriculum that the Greek and Latin classics had occupied, it was the usefulness of English as "an instrument of political education" that proved decisive. The partisans of English defeated the classicists not because anyone thought that English literature was intrinsically better on aesthetic grounds than the ancient classics; on the contrary, few thought it was. The decisive argument for English literature's curricular centrality was not its intrinsic value but the fact that it was English. The notion of relevance has come into disrepute since the sixties, but it was precisely the relevance of English to the needs and interests of English-speaking peoples that enabled it to triumph over Latin and Greek. This is not to say that questions of aesthetic value played no role, but rather that no great distinction was made between aesthetic and social value.

It was cultural nationalism that enabled English to move to the center of the college and school curriculum and led the other early departments of language and literature to be founded on national lines. It is thanks to nineteenth-century cultural nationalism that we still teach literature in departments labeled "English," "French," "German," "Spanish," and "Slavic," though it was easy to forget this political motivation once national departments became accepted and routine and nationality began to seem a neutral principle of organization. Thus it tends not to occur to us today that once we call a subject "English" or "French" literature, we have already "politicized" it, for "English" and "French" derive from political, not aesthetic, categories.

Once English and other modern European literatures had won entry into the curriculum on nationalistic grounds, the precedent they set was soon invoked to justify the claims of American literature, still widely despised by patrician academics as a degenerate, inferior branch of English literature.[15] Again, the argument was political as much as aesthetic—though again it was often hard to tell the difference—with advocates arguing not that American literature was better than English literature but that it was more relevant to the needs of American students, who, after all, were not British. Even neoconservative critics sometimes concede that the academic legitimation of American literature played a significant role in the United States' achievement of the status of a major world power. As James Tuttleton writes in a recent issue of the *New Criterion,* the early scholarship that established American literature as an academic field was "in large part intended to claim for American literature a stature comparable to [America's] position as a military and economic power in the postwar world."[16]

American literature study received a decisive boost from the xenophobia unleashed by World War I, which inspired, in the words of Fred Lewis Pattee a leading Americanist from Pennsylvania State University, "a kind of educational Monroe doctrine, for Americans American literature." Adhering to this doctrine himself in a school textbook, Pattee wrote that "more and more clearly it is seen now that the American soul, the American conception of democracy,—Americanism, should be made prominent in our school and college curriculums, as a guard against the rising spirit of experimental lawlessness which has followed the great war. . . ."[17] The concern with preaching "Americanism" and controlling "lawlessness" again suggest the unabashed extent to which the teaching of literature was conceived as "an instrument of political education."

Even more significantly, perhaps, those courses in the great books of Western civilization that are so widely adduced today as models of how culture transcends politics owe their very founding to the propaganda needs of World War I and its aftermath. The pilot Western civilization courses actually bore the title "War Issues" and were frankly designed to enhance the morale of students in training for combat by demonstrating the moral superiority of the Allies over Germans and later Bolsheviks. As one instructor, Dean Albert Kerr Heckel of Lafayette College, put it in 1918, "we were advised not to make the course one of propaganda, and yet it could not escape being propaganda. . . ."[18] Dean Herbert E. Hawkes, a founder of Columbia College's contemporary civilization course, described the aim of the course in 1925 as silencing the "destructive element in our society" by preparing students to "meet the arguments of the opponents of decency and sound government," thus making the student "a citizen who shall be safe for democracy."[19]

According to the historian Carol S. Gruber, who has studied course lectures extant in archives, Edward R. Turner, an instructor at the University of Michigan, lectured his students that "the German people do not have the humanitarian spirit of fair play, which the English, American and French do have. . . ."[20] William A. Frayer, another instructor at Michigan, remarked after the war on "the wild excesses of the revolutionists" in Russia, noting that "a surprising number" of them were Jews and warning that Bolsheviks were everywhere, even "on the campus of the University of Michigan."[21] The popular English professor who instituted the great books course at Berkeley, Charles Mills Gayley, published a treatise demonstrating "that Shakespeare's political philosophy . . . was that of the founders of liberty in America, was that of the Declaration of Independence."[22]

Again, the point is not that the great books courses were or are nothing but instruments of chauvinistic social control but that political concerns have intermingled in the planning of courses, the shaping of canons, and the judgments of intellectual and literary greatness. To put it more specifically, the apparent representativeness of a text—its ability to make readers feel that it somehow speaks for a whole nation or social group—has been an important component of intellectual and literary value. Their representative "Americanness" has been considered a key part of the literary value of classics like *The Last of the Mohicans,* Emerson's essays, *The Scarlet Letter, Walden, Moby-Dick, The Adven-*

tures of Huckleberry Finn, and *The Great Gatsby.* The blurb for a popular paperback edition describes *Moby-Dick,* for example, as "a parable of America's particular destiny"[23]; another blurb for an edition of James Fenimore Cooper's *The Prairie* states that "we still read Cooper today because he was the first of our authors to seize upon the dramatic possibilities of that unfallen western world that stands at the beginning of our national life."[24] Implicit in such praise is that some part of the aesthetic excellence of these works lies in their ability to convey a national group's particular experience. The same assumption underlies themes such as "the American dream" and "the quest for American identity," standard organizing principles of American literature and history courses.

During the period when the United States was still struggling to achieve a distinct cultural identity in the eyes of the world, literary critics both in and out of the academy did not hesitate to employ an unabashedly nationalistic rhetoric. But once this struggle had been won, the critics not only had the luxury to disavow this no-longer-needed rhetoric but could now scold excluded groups for being so presumptuous as to try to follow in the majority's footsteps.

The African-American literature critic Henry Louis Gates points out that when James Weldon Johnson made the case for the existence of an Afro-American poetry canon in the twenties, he invoked the same nationalistic principle that had been used to legitimate the establishment of the English and American literary canon. Johnson, as editor of *The Book of American Negro Poetry,* wrote that "the final measure of the greatness of all peoples is the amount and standard of the literature and art that they have produced."[25] The criterion of group expression that had legitimated the American canon was considered perverse and offensive, however, when used to justify the expression of minority cultures. And today when blacks, third world people, and others invoke the representation of group experience to claim value for their own literatures, they are reproved for replacing literary value with politics and demographic clout. It is a classic case of pulling the ladder up behind us once we have made it ourselves.

The rule seems to be that any politics is suspect except the kind that helped us get where we are, which by definition does not count as politics. Here is the double standard that governs recent attacks on political correctness: *Our* subjects earned their way into the curriculum on their own merits, but *theirs* are getting in only through political pressure, on a free handout or dole.

Putting Down Politics

CONSIDERING the low view of politics assumed by the attackers of political correctness, and considering their refusal to acknowledge any politics of their own, it follows that merely to call any piece of teaching or scholarship "politicized" is sufficient to discredit it without the need for further argument or explanation. So it is not surprising that, as Michael Kinsley observes in the *New Republic*, "many anti-PC diatribes are just lists of things the writer finds objectionable and would like—in the spirit of toleration and free inquiry—to expunge from the college curricula."[26] In these attacks it is often considered sufficient simply to *name* a particular practice, as if its perversity were self-evident. Thus *Time* magazine, in an article entitled "Upside Down in the Groves of Academe," complains that courses and reading lists today are frequently wedded "to outlandish views of the nation's culture and values" and that values are being taught "that are almost a reverse image of the American mainstream. As a result, a new intolerance is on the rise."[27] This sounds shocking until one reflects that "outlandish views" and challenges to the "American mainstream" are precisely what would reasonably be expected in a good teacher. A challenge to the American mainstream would constitute "intolerance" only to someone who thinks the function of education is simply to rubber-stamp mainstream values. Such statements lend credence to critic Michael Bérubé's observation that what angers conservatives is their failure "to achieve the kind of dominance in American universities that they now enjoy in most other arenas of American life."[28]

The intention of these preemptive strikes against "outlandish views" is evidently to make these views seem preposterous before anyone has a chance to understand exactly what they are. This effect is achieved by basing charges on incidents the critic does not claim to have investigated or verified or on the titles of articles or courses that he or she does not claim to have read or attended. In the most notable instance I know of this labor-saving practice, an essay was actually ridiculed in print not only before the critic had read it but before it had even been *written*. According to Eve Sedgwick of Duke University, Roger Kimball's attack on her conference paper, "Jane Austen and the Masturbating Girl," appeared in the *New Criterion* before she had got around to writing it. Mere nonexistence did not prevent Sedgwick's essay from becoming a central exhibit in countless subsequent anti-PC articles, and it still remains largely unread now that it has been published.[29]

Another anti-PC tactic is to make an argument *sound* scandalous by nothing more than the scornful tone in which it is described. Numerous national magazine articles have repeated Dinesh D'Souza's story of Duke English Professor Frank Lentricchia, who shows the film *The Godfather* in order to teach his students "that organized crime is 'a metaphor for American business as usual.' "[30] How disgraceful, you think—until you reflect that something along those lines *is* more or less the message of *The Godfather* (book and movie both), as it is the message of countless other celebrated films and literary works. In another instance of the double standard, the same ideas that have become respectable and even celebrated in the arts themselves are treated as outrageous when they are summarized by professors.

It would be tedious to try to document all the attacks on

politically oriented literary theories and approaches that could not conceivably be based on any firsthand knowledge of their subject. Attacks on deconstruction, for example, have come routinely from writers who have never read the work of Jacques Derrida and Paul de Man and haven't a clue to what deconstruction is about. (The determined anti-PC warrior is not deterred by the knowledge that he has no clue to what something is about; after acknowledging that he finds Derrida incomprehensible, Joseph Epstein proceeds to ridicule deconstruction for saying, supposedly, "that literature [is] itself inherently false, corrupt, in need of destruction."[31]) As Bérubé points out, since their targets are rarely accorded the privilege of responding to their attacks, such critics "feel entitled to say anything at all about the academy without fear of contradiction by general readers. The field is wide open, and there's no penalty for charlatanism (quite the contrary), since few general readers are informed enough to spot even the grossest forms of misrepresentation and fraud."[32]

These tactics are very effective, however, in conveying the impression that no political critic has ever had a thought that was not doctrinaire, reductive, and nihilistic. Here is George Will, in a widely discussed *Newsweek* essay subtitled " 'The Tempest'? It's 'Really' about Imperialism. Emily Dickinson's Poetry? Masturbation": ". . . academic Marxists deny the autonomy of culture, explaining it as a 'reflection' of other forces, thereby draining culture of its dignity. The reduction of literature to sociology, and of sociology to mere ideological assertion, has a central tenet: All literature is, whether writers are conscious of it or not, political."[33] Again, only if you stop to think will it occur to you that the beliefs being ridiculed might not seem obviously absurd if you knew precisely what they were.

Replying to Will, Michael Kinsley remarks that "anyone sensible denies the autonomy of culture."[34] "Autonomy" being the slippery concept that it is, however, the proposition "Culture is autonomous" is one on which it is probably unwise to take a true-false test. Few current politically oriented critics, Marxist or otherwise, actually *do* deny the autonomy of culture; they speak, rather, with Raymond Williams, Fredric Jameson, and Terry Eagleton, of culture's limited but significant autonomy within its own sphere. Indeed, one reason for the notorious difficulty of today's politically oriented criticism is its habit of going out of its way *not* to repeat the crudities perpetrated by the Marxists of the 1930s and the New Leftists of the 1960s, who often did reduce artworks to a mere "reflection" of class interests and ideologies, praising or damning them accordingly. In *The Political Unconscious,* probably the most influential work of academic political criticism in the 1980s, Jameson bends so far backward to avoid predictably reducing ideas to expressions of social class interest that he finds even in fascism a certain "utopian" dimension, monstrously perverted.[35]

In this respect Jameson is not as far as he may seem from Orwell, who sought to negotiate a middle ground between those who refused to see that art is political and those who refused to see that it is anything else. As I noted earlier, the most influential trend in today's politically oriented academic criticism is to see works of art not as simple ideological statements but as scenes of ideological and psychological conflict. There is a good deal of crudely reductive political criticism, but it is increasingly on the defensive within the camp of academic political critics themselves. Slogans that supposedly epitomize the movement like "Hey, hey, ho, ho, Western culture's gotta go" and "Dead White Males" would get you laughed out of most academic conferences. Anti-PC writers fail to understand that the professionalized academy above all values *sophistication,* a fact that limits the influence of simple doctrinaire arguments.

Oblivious of such niceties, popular critics of multiculturalism define the phenomenon as "an orthodoxy that prefers those texts that are racially pure," to quote the editors of the *New Republic.*[36] There *is* an ethnic purist or separatist wing in the multiculturalist movement, but it has been widely criticized within the movement itself, from which have come many critiques of "essentialism" and "identity politics"—the idea that our sex, race, gender, or class position determines how we think or write. If there is an emerging orthodoxy among multiculturalists—as a modest bit of reading in the writings of Gates, Houston A. Baker, Gayatri Spivak, James Clifford, and Edward Said would show— it is that racial purity is a myth.[37]

Novelist Toni Morrison sums up what has become the sophisticated view when she writes that "it does not 'go without saying' that a work written by an Afro-American is automatically subsumed by an enforcing Afro-American presence. There is a clear flight from blackness in a great deal of Afro-American lit- erature. In others there is the duel with blackness, and in some cases, as they say, 'You'd never know.' "[38] Morrison's point is that racial and ethnic distinctions are never pure but that as products of systematic oppression and violence these distinc- tions cannot simply be wished away. By not reading the best work on the opposing side, the anti-PC critics are missing out on critiques that are considerably more powerful than their own.

If it can be summed up in a phrase, the message of current academic political criticism is not that art is or should be an expression of ideological or racial purity but that art is a field of conflicts in which ideological factors play a major role that has been neglected. The Renaissance scholar Stephen Greenblatt makes the point in a response to Will's *Newsweek* article, explaining why the application of political categories to Shake- speare is legitimate:

[T]he student of Shakespeare who asks about racism, misogyny, or anti-Semitism is not on the slippery slope toward what George Will calls "collective amnesia and deculturation." He or she is on the way to understanding something about *Othello, The Taming of the Shrew,* and *The Merchant of Venice.* It is, I believe, all but impossible to understand these plays without grappling with the dark energies upon which Shakespeare's art so powerfully draws. And it is simi- larly difficult to come to terms with what *The Tempest* has to teach us about forgiveness, wisdom, and social atonement if we do not also come to terms with its relation to colonialism.[39]

Note that Greenblatt does not claim that *The Merchant of Venice* or *The Tempest* is a simple expression of anti-Semitism or colonialism. He sees these plays as arenas of conflict between these "dark energies" and more positive impulses. Nor does Greenblatt urge shifting attention from the literary aspects of *The Merchant of Venice* and *The Tempest* to their assumptions about human differences and social authority. His point is that these political assumptions are part of what gives the plays their literary power.

There is ample textual support for Greenblatt's point. From the opening scene of *The Tempest,* in which sailors and aristocrats bicker over who should be in charge of a storm-tossed ship, the play is concerned at virtually every moment with questions of usurpation, loyalty, deference, precedence—of who has title over whom and who has the right to order whom to do what. At several points the bestial Caliban protests that he has been dispossessed of the island paradise in which the play is set and reduced to slavery by Prospero, the play's central figure, who embodies European power and intelligence (though, to complicate things further, Prospero is himself a dispossessed prince). Caliban challenges Prospero directly, making the issue of power and usurpation explicit:

> This island's mine by Sycorax my mother,
> Which thou taks't from me.[40]

Later Caliban cries that he is "subject to a tyrant, a sorcerer, that by his cunning hath cheated me of the island."

Caliban is called a liar, first by Prospero himself, then by Prospero's spirit Ariel, both of whom seem to speak for Shakespeare himself. The scenes in which Caliban asserts his rights appear meant to be played as comic interludes, as if the grievances of such subhuman figures were not to be taken seriously.

Yet the effect of Caliban's complaints is to make us reflect on the European cultural superiority that Shakespeare otherwise seems comfortably to presuppose. "I do not lie," Caliban says at one point. "I say by sorcery [Prospero] got this isle; from me he got it. . . ."[41] Since it *was* through sorcery that Prospero gained control of the island, Caliban's charge that he has been dispossessed cannot quite be dismissed as the bit of farce seemingly intended.

Greenblatt and other recent new historicists argue that this contradiction in *The Tempest*—the simultaneous acceptance of Caliban's suppression and the invitation to see it as injustice— reflects the social changes and anxieties of Shakespeare's world. More precisely, the play does not "reflect" these changes and anxieties (as an older Marxist critic might have said) but was and may still be an active agent in producing these cultural attitudes. Caliban and other lower-class figures in Shakespeare's plays resemble the so-called masterless men who began to appear in the London streets in the late decades of Elizabeth's reign and aroused the concern of social authorities. The preoccupation with the social problem of the masterless man became part of a larger Renaissance debate over the morality of burgeoning Western colonialism and its enslavement of subject populations.

Earlier scholars and critics had noticed a connection between the dispossession of Caliban from his island and the colonialist initiative in the New World that was in full swing in 1611, when *The Tempest* is thought to have been first performed. In fact, D. H. Lawrence touched on the imperialist connection in 1923 in his *Studies in Classic American Literature,* where he quoted (actually misquoted) a snatch of one of Caliban's songs as a foreshadowing of the liberatory energies of the New World:

> 'Ban, 'Ban, Ca-Caliban
> Has a new master. Get a new man![42]

Lawrence saw that *The Tempest* is bursting with rebellious political impulses—the impulse to "be masterless"—that Shakespeare does not approve but whose excitement he identifies with.[43]

Will might reply to Greenblatt by asking how, if it is "all but impossible" to understand *The Tempest* without grappling with racism and colonialism, have so many people seemed to understand the play quite well without even being aware of such issues, much less grappling with them. Greenblatt might retort that if audiences and readers have paid little attention to these issues, this tells us less about the play than about the restricted definition of "the literary" that has come to be accepted in the modern era. Shakespeare's audience may have found it easier than we do to see the political ramifications of *The Tempest* because there was as yet no doctrine that opposed the theatrical to the political; indeed, the theater was a form of political spectacle that has only subsequently been divorced from its original social context and turned into an aesthetic object. He might also add that insofar as audiences become familiar with recent interpretations, these political ramifications figure to inform their responses—as they do in Latin American countries, where *The Tempest* has frequently been staged (or rewritten) as a play about colonialism.[44]

When Is a Side Not a Side?

WE are accustomed to thinking of politics and ideology as either part of the explicit message of literature or not there at all. When we think of politics in literature, we think of the overt anti-Semitism in Ezra Pound's "Pisan Cantos" or the explicit critique of totalitarianism in Orwell's *Nineteen Eighty-four*. But as Orwell pointed out in "Politics and the English Language," political assumptions influence us all the more deeply when they are not stated in openly propagandistic terms.[45] That is, literature acts politically on us even when it is not explicitly *about* topics traditionally defined as political. As the critic Gregory Jay puts it, " 'politics' crops up in literature whenever characterizing assumptions are made about sexes, races, and other groupings, not just when a text is about kings or wars or a labor-strike."[46]

In this broad sense of the term, politics is involved whenever a text makes assumptions about what kind of sexuality is normal and abnormal, what kind of social order is good or bad, and which social groups have the right to run things. Politics lies in what is taken for granted as going without saying—as Milton takes it for granted in *Paradise Lost* that Eve is mentally inferior to Adam or as Tom Wolfe—in my reading of the book any-way—takes it for granted in *The Bonfire of the Vanities* that blacks will run wild if the whites who naturally run society do not have the courage to control them.

Again a double standard is at work. Change is political, but keeping things as they are is not. A status quo that we are used to and comfortable with is not seen as political; one who says, "Western culture has made the world we know and therefore should be preeminent in the curriculum," is seen simply as stating a *fact,* not endorsing an agenda. Like the oxygen that we notice only when it is taken away, the orthodox or established side does not stand out from its background and seems therefore not to be a "side" at all but just the way things are.

Nigerian novelist Chinua Achebe puts the point another way when he argues that a novel can never be politically neutral because "even the attempt to say nothing about politics is a big political statement. You are saying, then, that everything is OK." It is not a question, Achebe says, of writing "bad and tedious political treatises." But in the West "if you say that a novel is political it's almost like saying it's no good," for Western "novelists and poets have bought the idea that it's not really their business to examine political realities. . . ."[47] One effect of bringing non-Western traditions into the curriculum would be to challenge the narrowly provincial concept of the political that passes for common sense in the West.

Achebe's point is that what a text does not say can be as tendentious as what it explicitly says. Like any argument based on identifying what is supposedly "repressed" from a text, this one is open to abuse. But this does not change the fact that politically significant omissions do take place and that one doesn't have to be a radical to engage in "demystifying" them. Conservatives practice the demystification of repressed ideology every time they attack leftist critics of capitalism for their silence about the sins of socialism.

One can only admire the conservatives' skill, however, in conveying the impression—and evidently believing it themselves—that it is only their leftist opponents in the culture war who are being "political," that indeed, it is only the left that even *has* a politics, much less a humorlessly "correct" politics. Thus George Will can denounce the "politicization of higher education" without seeing anything political in his own view that the function of literature is to be the "social cement" that unites us as a common culture.[48] In a similar way, NEH Chairman Cheney (for whom Will has become a publicist) can at one moment boast of being a "conservative populist"[49] and deplore "the radical anti-Americanism" of her critics and at the next call for "the depoliticizing and deideologizing" of the humanities.[50] When the Modern Language Association opposed the nomination of Carol Iannone to Cheney's advisory council in 1991,Cheney denounced its action as politically motivated even though Iannone would never have been nominated at all had she not been a savage critic of feminism and other current trends. As Richard Cohen observed in a *Washington Post* editorial, "had Iannone written brilliantly in defense of feminism, Cheney would have looked elsewhere."[51] Cheney has subsequently intensified the packing of her advisory council with ideological cronies, discouraging controversial scholarship in much the same way the National Endowment for the Arts has begun to discourage controversial art.

It is noteworthy that those who complain most loudly about the intrusion of politics into literature classrooms are not troubled when professors of economics, management, law, and political science routinely take for granted the sanctity of the free market and the virtuousness of American domestic and military policy. None of these critics have come forward to protest the fact that the so-called Law and Economics movement has become one of the dominant theories in major law schools, even though the movement has been described sympathetically as "the legal expression of the Reagan administration's economic theories" and a theory that "fit Reaganomics like a glove."[52]

The journalist Robert Kuttner has argued that economics departments have been dominated by a far more monolithic and pervasive "tyranny of the economically correct" than anything seen in the humanities. "To be credentialed to practice economics today," Kuttner writes, "one must accept a certain corpus of theology" in which the law of supply and demand is absolute, and "efforts to interfere with this natural order of things, notably governments, are damaging to economic efficiency and, hence, bad." I am hardly qualified to judge, but I have even heard it suggested that some of America's present economic difficulties might have been averted if departments of economics had been more open to criticism of their assumption that dire consequences follow from governmental tampering with free markets. In any case, Kuttner argues that by comparison with economics, "other academic disciplines are rich with healthy contention, in ideology, assumption, and method."[53]

To make sure things stay this way, an impressive interlocking network of right-wing foundations such as the Olin Foundation, the American Enterprise Institute, and the Hudson Institute has been spending millions of dollars to establish conservative centers and institutes in major universities in the fields of law, economics, government, and political science. Olin also funds the National Association of Scholars, an extensive chain of conservative campus newspapers, including the virulently racist *Dartmouth Review,* and ideologically congenial spokesmen like William Bennett and Allan Bloom. Former *Dartmouth Review* editor Dinesh D'Souza's *Illiberal Education* was written on a grant from the American Enterprise Institute and promoted with another grant from Olin. Organizations like Olin make no secret of their goal of reversing the gains of multiculturalism and affirmative action and returning education to "traditional values," yet this agenda and its formidable financial backing have at this writing still escaped the general label of "politicization" that the press attaches to its targets of criticism.[54]

Much has been written about the leftist leanings of certain members of the Duke University English department, but very little about the three-quarters of a million dollars with which Olin has endowed programs in "Normative Economy" in the Duke political science department and law and economics in the Duke School of Law. The alleged harassment by black students of Harvard history Professor Stephan Thernstrom was the subject of a sensational cover story for *New York* magazine,[55] which was then cited widely as an archetypal instance of the PC juggernaut, though it now appears that the accusations against the students were wildly exaggerated.[56] But little attention has been given to the Harvard Law School's receipt of $1,645,000 from the Olin Foundation for another program in law and economics.

On the rare occasions when a conservative acknowledges he is indeed acting politically, it is allegedly only in order to eliminate politics from the scene. This disarming claim has been made by Harvey C. Mansfield, one of the numerous conservatives with whom Lynne Cheney, notwithstanding her setback in the Iannone case, has packed her advisory council to the National Endowment for the Humanities. "It's ironic," said Mansfield, as quoted by the *Chronicle of Higher Education,* "that conservatives have to use politics to rid the campus of politics, but we do." Unlike their leftist opponents, whose commitment to politics is merely self-interested, Mansfield and his colleagues will engage in politics only in order to remove it from the educational scene, not to serve any interests of their own. It sounds very disinterested, but can you really "use politics to rid the campus of politics" without politicizing the campus in your own way and for your own purposes? With admirable candor about how he proposes to use politics to end politics, Mansfield has vowed, according to the *Chronicle,* that in his role on the council "I'm going to use a West Point approach and sound the guns against those in the humanities who want to destroy the greatness of our intellectual past."[57]

Instead of contorting themselves in such grotesque feats of doublethink, one wonders why the conservatives do not give up the pretense and say what they often seem really to mean, which is something like: "Yes, *of course,* we, too, are being 'political' about literature and the arts. But our conservative cultural politics are *better* than your liberal or radical politics. Our politics are better because they are better grounded in the realities of American life and global development." This would be fair, however disputable, and it might advance the debate that is really at the center of the culture war, over competing political visions of education. Some such avowal—we, too, are being political, but our politics are better than yours—seems all but explicit in the many attacks in right-wing journals like *Commentary,* the *New Criterion,* and the *American Scholar* on "anti-Americanism" in fiction writers like E. L. Doctorow, Norman Mailer, Philip Roth, and Thomas Pynchon or in the latest show at the Museum of Modern Art or the latest work of academic art history.

Of course, an acknowledgment by the right that it, too, has a political stake in the discussion would forfeit the strategic advantage of pretending to be above politics. On the other hand, the controversies over the curriculum and political correctness may be making it harder for the right to maintain the pretense. If so, it may soon become possible to move the debate beyond its present phase, in which buzzwords like "politicize" and "ideology" are endlessly lobbed back and forth across the trenches.

I have argued that politics have always played a major role in the teaching of literature, not least when literary study has presented itself as transcending politics. I do not minimize, however, the serious problems for students posed by the more and more openly politicized condition of the academy. This brings us back to John Searle's argument that "where possible the professor should leave his or her political views out of the class-room." Such an argument seems to me unhelpful in an academic climate where there is serious controversy over what should and should not count as a "political view" and where the prospect of authorities policing the distinction is not attractive.

It is just as unhelpful, however, to answer critics like Searle by reiterating slogans like "all teaching is political," as if such a point had already been explained and demonstrated. The Marx-ist critic Terry Eagleton has observed that "in the critique of ideology, only those interventions will work which make sense to the mystified subject"[58]—that is those not on the left. Yet little recent ideological criticism even tries to make a sense to such people, much less to respect their objections as arguments need-ing to be addressed rather than as mere mystifications. The same problem holds for the growing body of writing that calls for an oppositional curriculum, a transformative educational practice, a "pedagogy of the oppressed." This radical educational writing never stops to ask what is to be done with those teachers and students who do not wish to be radicalized.

A similar assumption of an already favorably predisposed constituency seems to characterize many of today's cultural studies programs, to the point that "cultural studies" has become a euphemism for leftist studies. Though cultural studies seems to me a highly promising umbrella-concept for connecting and integrating the disciplines, it can hardly serve that purpose— and it can certainly not live up to its democratic pretensions— if it excludes everyone from its orbit who does not already agree with leftist postulates about the political nature of culture. In short, if the left hopes to advance it must risk entering a debate that it would not necessarily be guaranteed to win.

My own solution is the one I have offered in other connec-tions throughout this book: The best way to prevent students from being bullied by their teachers' political views is to bring them into the debates between those views. Students are already being exposed to the violent ideological conflicts of the university every day, but they are exposed to these conflicts in conditions that not only make it difficult for them to join the discussion but create pressure to conform. Then, too, when there is little open debate, teachers readily project paranoid myths about one another, deepening the campus's atmosphere of suspicion and hostility. It may be difficult to eliminate political intimidation and paranoia completely, but a curriculum that presented students with an engagement between the contending political views to which they are exposed would do much to defuse them.

This solution will not satisfy those who want to return to an academic and social world whose politics were so uniform that they were not recognized as politics. But it should appeal to the many—left, right, and center—who no longer think that way. Instead of pretending we can eliminate political conflict from teaching, we should start making use of it. All the parties in the culture war claim to stand for democratic debate. They should be asked to prove it.

Chapter 9

Turning Conflict into Community

I START with three accounts of education when it has worked. The first is a recollection by the distinguished American literature scholar Leo Marx on joining the English department at the University of Minnesota in 1949. The scene in the department reflected a lively three-cornered debate that was emerging in English studies at the time, involving traditional literary historians, formalistic New Critics, and practitioners, like Marx, of the new field of American studies. Marx writes:

> [T]hough no programmatic effort was made to exploit our differences in designing the curriculum, we learned an immense amount from each other, and the students also benefited from our differences. No student could fail to be aware of the striking contrasts between what went on in our various classrooms, and the best students sampled courses offered by adherents of each group. . . .
> The result was to heighten everyone's awareness of the opposed ways of defining, enjoying, studying, and teaching literature. . . . [T]he mere presence of articulate exponents of rival theories . . . demonstrated the promising possibilities to be had from a policy of

teaching our differences. It lent a rare, invaluable intensity of phil-
osophic implication to the study of literature.[1]

My second account comes from a 1991 letter to the *Chronicle
of Higher Education* by Ron Hamberg, the dean of instruction at
Seattle Central Community College, describing the results of the
integrated curriculum at his college: "Imagine students who will
not leave the classroom at some fixed time. Imagine students
eagerly reading original source material, who seek out the library
for additional information to be used as ammunition in an
upcoming debate. Imagine students who seek out at home fellow team members who have missed a class session in order to
make certain that they will be coming to the next session. . . ."[2]

The third account comes from a student who went through
an integrated curriculum at the State University of New York at
Stony Brook: "[In this program] we never have to turn off one
idea and turn on another, as we travel the campus going from
class to class. Our minds are opened, formulating ideas and connecting all the disciplines."[3]

All three statements trace educational success to the ability of
an institution to create a community out of its differences. The
implied premise in each case, I think, is the one guiding me in
this book, that students need to experience an educational community in order to be able to join one. As I argued in Chapter 6
against educational critics on the right, until the components of
the curriculum are connected, it is difficult to make a fair assess-
ment of its potential. Integrating the curriculum attempts to give
academic culture a chance to work by connecting its dissociated
parts.

Such a strategy is both conservative and radical. It is conservative in its assumption that before educational institutions
completely abandon existing practices for something totally different, they should try to get more than they are getting out of
those practices by relating them. It is radical in that the effect
would be to make entrenched positions open to question, to

destabilize established views, and to tap a greater part of the enormous potential of our educational diversity.

Why Past Curricular Integration Has Failed

AS national attention highlights the frustration and anger at the more prestigious campuses, promising reforms have been quietly taking shape at places like Seattle Central Community College, largely unnoticed by the major institutions. This is not surprising, for the same factors that inhibit communication between courses and departments on one campus also inhibit communication between campuses. And even when major institutions are serious about curricular reform—as most now are—they are often too proud to learn from less prominent ones.

It is increasingly clear that the kind of intellectual community that took shape spontaneously at Minnesota in 1949 is not likely to happen today without what Leo Marx calls "programmatic effort." Intellectual and ideological hostilities are deeper now than they were then, there has been a vast multiplication of approaches and vocabularies in the disciplines, and the boundaries that once neatly separated the disciplines have been challenged and transgressed. The student body has also changed. Not only are there many more students, but they come from a wider range of backgrounds and attend community colleges like Dean Hamberg's which did not exist in 1949. These students arrive at college with fewer of the shared intellectual reference points possessed by Marx's generation. In these changed circumstances the kind of intellectual community Marx describes is unlikely to materialize by pure serendipity except perhaps in the smallest colleges. Something as complex as an intellectual culture will not organize itself intelligibly and usefully for students unless steps are taken to bring it about.

Consider how crucial it is in government agencies and busi-

nesses to coordinate the tasks of individual workers. Such institutions cannot afford to assume that if these workers function
effectively as individuals the combined result of their efforts will
take care of itself. Yet this has been the implicit assumption of
educational institutions, partly because they legitimately desire
to keep teaching free from excessive bureaucratic interference,
partly perhaps because the sheer diversity and complexity of a
modern faculty seem to thwart any attempt to organize its activities. For these and other reasons, educational institutions have
tended to favor a kind of invisible hand philosophy: Recruit
good teachers, turn them loose to do their stuff while encouraging course innovation, and the rest will take care of itself.

When it does not take care of itself and the educational results
are not what were hoped for, the failure tends to be blamed on
poor individual teaching, which is in turn traced to the lack of
rewards for good teaching and on interference from the pressures of research. Though often true as far as it goes, this diagnosis ignores the fact that a serious obstacle to good teaching
may be the poor organization of courses and subjects. Admirable as they may be, attempts to improve education by focusing
only on individual teaching tend to divert attention from larger
systematic factors and thus keep educational reform efforts limited and superficial. The most effective way to improve individual teaching, I believe, would be to provide it with a richer context
of relationships in which to work. This means developing a more
coherent curriculum.

It is possible, of course, that educational institutions have not
failed to recognize the importance of coordinating teaching, but
that bitter experience has convinced them that it cannot be done,
especially in the large bureaucratized multiversity. The idea of
an integrated curriculum is an old, unfulfilled dream of progres-
sive educational thinking. It was implicit in the educational vision
of John Dewey, who saw the limitations of a curriculum based
on decontextualized subjects abstracted from their social setting.
For Dewey, the modern conception of the curriculum as "a kind

of composite made by the aggregation of segregated values" was a symptom of "the isolation of social groups and classes" in society at large. Dewey believed it was "the business of education in a democratic social group to struggle against this isolation in order that the various interests may reinforce and play into one another."[4]

The most famous early college experiment in curricular integration was carried out not by Dewey, however, but by the classicist Alexander Meiklejohn in his Experimental College at the University of Wisconsin in the 1920s. Meiklejohn's example inspired the Experimental Program at Berkeley in the mid-sixties, under the leadership of Joseph Tussman, and Tussman's work has in turn inspired several present-day programs, most notably at Evergreen State College in Olympia, Washington, whose principles we will look at in a moment.

The earliest attempts to integrate the curriculum were all short-lived, for reasons we need to understand if we are to avoid repeating their failures again today. An exemplary test case is the fate of the Berkeley Experimental Program, conveniently documented in Tussman's book *Experiment at Berkeley*. The Experimental Program was essentially a great books curriculum (though Tussman disclaimed the term[5]) with a heavy emphasis on ancient classics. The approximately 150 students who volunteered for the program over the three years of its existence agreed to renounce their freedom to choose elective options in order to take a "set and completely required" sequence of courses concentrating on the study of literary and philosophical classics. The program formed a close intellectual subcommunity created by students all taking the same courses and engaging regularly in intense small group discussions with the faculty. In this and other respects, the Experimental Program went against the grain of countercultural "student-centered" pedagogy at Berkeley. Indeed, there was a lockstep quality to the program's curriculum—Tussman himself described it as "overwhelming in its givenness"[6]—and this ultimately doomed it, limiting the number of students and professors to whom it could appeal.

In one respect Tussman and his associates did have something in common with the Berkeley radicals: a reaction against the large and impersonal research university. Tussman saw the Experimental Program as a means of reviving the integrity of the undergraduate liberal "college" against the professionalized research "university"—an attempt to strike a blow for general education against the drift of professional and vocational specialization.[7] Tussman conceded that similar attempts elsewhere to reinstate the spirit of the old liberal college had amounted to "a dispirited rearguard action against the triumphant university."[8] This posed a problem, as he acknowledged. The undergraduate college and the research-oriented university were not two separate groups of faculty but one: "[T]he men who are the university are also, however, the men who are the college."[9]

The question, however, was how, if the faculty was at least partly committed to the research university, the conflict was to be resolved on the side of the undergraduate college. Tussman never came up with a clear answer to this question. He nevertheless insisted that somehow the college "must make its stand."[10]

Tussman was caught in the same self-defeating logic that has plagued more conventional attempts to revive the unifying values of general education in a university increasingly committed to diverse interests and the questioning of traditional beliefs and to a research enterprise that reflects both impulses. Since Tussman regarded the research functions of the university as incompatible with the values of general education, his approach amounted to a defensive circling of the wagons. Conceived as a kind of throwback to earlier values, undergraduate education could only remain the quixotic lost cause of an embittered minority, which might gain a sense of moral superiority, but little else, by its defiance of the modern professional world. What did not occur to Tussman was that general education might be revitalized by being brought into *relation* with the research func-

tions of the university instead of trying to be a last-ditch coun-
terweight against them.

Generalizing from such cases, we can list three major factors
that seem to have prevented early attempts at curricular integration from becoming a general model for educational reform.

1. In these attempts, the goal of integrating the curriculum was confused with the goal of achieving a consensus on the fundamentals
   of knowledge. Achieving a *common* educational experience was confused with securing agreement on the values informing the experience. The common ground ended up being a narrow conception of
   the great books that, in fact, had ceased to be commonly shared, in
   either the academic world or the world outside.

2. Early attempts to integrate the curriculum failed to recruit faculty
   over a sustained period because in both their philosophy of education and the demands they put on the faculty they conflicted with
   the faculty's professional research obligations. This failure was then
   blamed on those research obligations, yet no effort had been made
   to encourage the faculty to integrate their research interests with
   the demands of their teaching. By assuming that research naturally
   conflicted with teaching, such programs made themselves dependent on the willingness of instructors to sacrifice their professional
   careers, as few were likely to do.

3. Early integrative programs had difficulty recruiting students for reasons similar to those that made it difficult for them to recruit faculty. Just as these programs asked the faculty to renounce its research
   interests, they asked the students to renounce their electives—which
   is to say, their interests in the world outside the confines of the
   program. The programs did create a common educational experience, but only by rigidly restricting the choices of the faculty and
   student body.

It was not just that the early experiments in curricular integration restricted teachers' and students' interests, however. At
a deeper level these experiments were out of step with both the
culture of the modern professional university and the rapidly
changing culture of American life. They sought an overarching
synthesis of knowledge and values that was incompatible with

the dynamism and dissonance of the twentieth century. In this respect, however, these integrative experiments were victims of the same anachronistic philosophy that still underlies most of our general education curricula today. General education has foundered because it has been conceived as a kind of compensation for the specialization of vocationalism and research, making it difficult to recruit faculty to teach general education courses and to stimulate enthusiasm in students for taking them.

Yet Meiklejohn and Tussman left a fruitful legacy. More recent institutions attempting curricular integration seem disposed to free the idea from their predecessors' hostility to modern professionalism and modern culture. What current experiments in curricular integration seem to have learned from their predecessors is the need to draw on the university's research culture instead of viewing that culture as an inherent source of corruption. Such an outlook has been made feasible by changes in the research culture (which I discussed in Chapter 6) that have made research less narrowly specialized than it was in the era of Dewey and Meiklejohn and perhaps even of Tussman.

Instead of straining, as Meiklejohn and Tussman had, to impose a unity on the curriculum from the top, the programs that seem most promising to me seek their principles of curricular coherence in the already existing practices, interactions, and debates of the disciplines. Instead of a last-ditch effort to "make a stand" for the college and teaching against research, these programs look for ways to integrate these perennial antagonists. Instead of confusing curricular coherence with consensus, these programs aim to inject common experience into the curriculum without assuming the need for a consensus on values and beliefs.[11]

Curricular Integration Today

INTEGRATIVE programs across the country are now so numerous and proliferating so rapidly that it is possible to mention only a fraction of them here. These programs are usually interdisciplinary, for curricular integration tends to go hand in hand with the interdisciplinary movement, though it is possible to apply integrative principles within a department without moving across disciplines, and in some cases this may be the most practical first step. The Association for Integrative Studies, headquartered at Western College of Miami University in Oxford, Ohio, publishes a newsletter on interdisciplinary education and has produced a useful *Directory of Interdisciplinary Programs.*[12] A book entitled *Learning Communities,* by Faith Gabelnick, Jean MacGregor, Roberta S. Matthews, and Barbara Leigh Smith, surveys the different kinds of integrative programs and their principles. It would provide an excellent sourcebook for any college wishing to review the present range of curricular integration efforts.[13]

The basic pedagogical strategy of integrated curricula adapts and goes beyond the principle of team teaching, which places two or more instructors in the same course. The simplest form of integrative structure (and therefore the easiest and cheapest to institutionalize and administer) is probably the jointly taught introductory course, which aims to provide concepts and contexts that students can use to connect other courses in the program. At Wright State University of Dayton, Ohio, for example, the standard sophomore survey of English and American literature is taught by "virtually the entire full-time English staff with a specialist in each literary period doing a one- or two-day stint covering his or her particular field." According to an article on the course by a member of the department, Lawrence Hussman, this device "stimulates dialogue and debate among the faculty members and . . . allows the students to recognize and begin to participate"[14] in them.

The interplay of faculty perspectives in the course, according to Hussman, helps students "see the logical development of literary history as well as the warring ways of approaching it, the continuity and the conflict. The coherent pattern of that history emerges when students study in sequence, for example, English neoclassicism and pre-Romanticism."[15] At the same time students also begin to appreciate central disagreements and to be more critical of prevailing categories, developing "a healthy disrespect for 'isms,' 'istics,' and 'ists' . . . that does not nullify the necessity of knowing the categories and their contexts."[16] A student who took the course compared it favorably with previous survey courses, in which he had "always had trouble keeping the periods straight. It really helps to identify the different authors and periods with the different professors."[17] Another said that because of the faculty interplay, "this course really kept my interest better than any other I've taken at the university."[18]

A more informal kind of integrated teaching that accomplishes some of the same ends as the jointly taught course at Wright State can be practiced by two or more instructors exchanging classes periodically or meeting their classes jointly on scheduled occasions staggered over the semester to discuss a common text. This "teacher-swapping" device, as I have called it,[19] is both less expensive and less labor-intensive than team teaching and perhaps less prone to reproduce student passivity. By periodically exchanging classes, the teachers not only bring fresh perspectives into one another's courses but also create situations which enable them to use one another's interests as contexts to refer to and play off of. Since the teacher coming in from outside is largely ignorant of what has been going on in the class, he or she is in a better position than the "home" teacher to ask the students to summarize and reinterpret the point of the course, usually a valuable exercise.

A more ambitious and complex form of integration than either teacher swapping or the staff-taught introductory course involves the clustering of several courses, the basic tactic of the "learning communities" approach. The authors of the book of that title define a "learning community" as a curricular structure formed by the integration of several courses (usually but not necessarily from different disciplines) around a common theme.[20] This strategy takes advantage of the many common issues shared by courses and departments that go unexploited and unrecognized in the conventional curriculum. Learning community clusters have proved especially effective in introductory courses, in freshman composition (where they are often part of a Writing Across the Curriculum program), and in general education courses. An advantage of the thematic cluster is that it is compatible with the traditional departmental structure even as it permits faculty from different departments to teach together.

Learning Communities describes programs in which courses in the sciences and humanities are brought together around the themes of "Human Nature," "Science, Technology, and Human Values," and "The City," to explore major ethical and social questions.[21] In another program, courses in general management, introduction to philosophy, and speech are merged around the theme of "Law in Nature, Society, and Language." In still another, the theme of "The American Myth of Success" brings together courses in management, composition, and film, presumably to compare critiques and defenses of American individualism.[22] Here are two typical learning community clusters at Seattle Community College and Bellevue Community College in the state of Washington:

"Power and the Person: Looking at the Renaissance": This cluster compares "three periods of re-awakening: the 15th century European Renaissance, the Harlem Renaissance of the 1920s and 30s, and the American upheavals of the 1960s." Combines instructors of English, music history, art, and history.

"Science Shakes the Foundations: Dickens, Darwin, Marx, and You": A cluster taught jointly by professors of English, physical anthropology, and political economy that examines "19th century views of evolution and how they inform the way we see the world."[23] Like the "renaissance" theme, this one brings out historical contrasts and continuities that are usually obscured.

The interdisciplinary integrated studies program at the University of Missouri—Kansas City has developed learning community clusters of two to four courses on common themes and historical periods. "All of the courses within a cluster meet together for at least one third of the sessions in order to ensure a fruitful cross-fertilization of ideas," though since each faculty member still teaches a separate course, the program fits the usual administrative calculus for crediting faculty time. Several of the clusters have focused on a particular historical period: "Kingship in the Middle Ages," bringing together courses in English, history, and philosophy; "Images of the Human Body in the Renaissance" (art history, English, history). Other clusters have centered on themes such as "Law and Society through Film," which brings together courses in business and public administration and English.[24]

Two of the program's instructors, Susan L. Feagin and Burton L. Dunbar, write that working together in these courses enabled faculty to grow out of "narrow and specialized teaching. When we are required to assimilate material from other disciplines into the context of a course, we are forced to reexamine the ways in which our own disciplines relate to other fields of scholarship and to the humanities in general. The difficulties many of us have in communicating with colleagues in other departments give new insight into how difficult it must be for uninitiated *students* to appreciate what we are trying to do."[25] Faculty members working in the clusters, according to Feagin and Dunbar, thought that "observing the pedagogical techniques of others refreshed their own teaching methods and often "new research ideas emerged from the contact." Though the abundance of viewpoints was confusing to some students, "most saw it as challenging and stimulating," with some 80 percent of students surveyed afterward saying they would elect cluster courses instead of "normal" ones. A typical student comment was: "I find I learn something better when I can relate it to other fields of study."[26] According to Gabelnick and her colleagues, faculty members in learning communities claim that a higher proportion of students become independent, self-motivated, and willing to try out intellectual styles. Teachers feel able to "demand more in these programs, and get more in terms of student perseverance and quality of performance."[27] The English major at the University of Chicago will be experimenting with thematic clusters this year.

One of the original programs discussed by Gabelnick and her coauthors was established in 1976 at the State University of New York at Stony Brook under the name Federated Learning Communities (FLC). It was founded by Patrick J. Hill, a philosophy professor who subsequently became provost at Evergreen State College, an institution influenced by Joseph Tussman's work at Berkeley. Hill writes that the FLC idea first arose out of dissatisfaction with the isolation of the established curriculum, in which, according to Hill, the chance for students to see "experts in conflict over subject matter and methodology is *announced* in the atomistic curriculum but seldom exhibited. . . ."[28] Hill and five associates selected six existing courses in the catalog that spanned the standard divisions of the humanities and physical and social sciences and "federated" them into "two continuous thematically coherent semesters." The six courses supported one another "with a common focus, shared language, somewhat overlapping reading material, and common reference points. . . ."[29]

FLC students, who included humanities, social science, and natural science majors, volunteered to take all six courses over a three-semester period, along with the other students who happened to enroll in one or more of the courses. The six federated faculties convened once a month with the FLC students during the three semesters in a special core course, in which "the most sustained attention [was] given both to the theme of the program and to the nature and interrelationship of the federated disciplines."[30]

A further innovation was the use of a so-called Master Learner, a faculty member who "took" the FLC courses and acted as a mediator between faculty and students, during which time he was relieved from normal teaching duties. The Master Learners were "interpreters or mediators" between faculty and students and vice versa; their role was to "explain the expectations of students to the faculty and the expectations of faculty to the students. The Master Learners, more importantly, assist faculty and students in seeing values in those expectations that might not otherwise be perceived."[31]

Hill claims—and Stony Brook graduates I have spoken to corroborate his account—that the FLC program produced a discernible increase in students' interest in academic work and in readiness to take responsibility for their studies. Hill stresses the valuable "relativizing" effect of FLC, in which students recognized that knowledge is not a set of inert contents to be passively accepted but is *"relative* to particular inquiries."[32] In FLC "the students thus become resources for the further education of the faculty. . . ."[33] Yet the spirit of FLC bore little resemblance to the facile relativism that holds that any context or set of readings is as good as any other or to the touchy-feely abrogation of professorial authority that vitiated many of the educational experiments of the sixties. The effect of FLC was not to relax rigor and standards but to make education *more* rigorous, by asking students to take an active part in disciplinary and interdisciplinary conversations they are usually not expected to take part in.

Hill concedes that "many students cannot cope with the phenomenon of their teachers disagreeing or of a Core course meeting that produces no 'answer.' "[34] Students who have become accustomed to waiting for their teachers to pump out formulary answers to questions are indeed likely to feel anxious in the more freewheeling and less predictable discussions of FLC and other learning communities. On the other hand, anyone who grows up in the contemporary United States cannot be a total stranger to ambiguity and dissonance. As the increasing unpredictability of modern culture and of modern work makes education based on prepackaged answers less and less useful, students figure to recognize that the skills of analysis and argumentation emphasized by learning communities are by no means impractical.

What is not easy for an outsider to judge is the extent to

which the FLC experience made a crucial difference to students. Though Hill acknowledges that the FLC program at Stony Brook was aimed at more mature students, he claims that the effectiveness of the model is by no means limited to students who come to college already disposed to academic forms of intellectuality. He argues, in fact, that students who are disaffected from the intellectual life tend to thrive all the more on the FLC model. Gabelnick and her colleagues claim that far from being effective only in small or elite colleges, as one might expect, learning communities have proven "particularly valuable in large institutions and commuter campuses, where close personal contacts and community-making are problematic at best"[35]

There is ample data now available assessing the success of learning communities, and the portion that I have examined tends to bear out these claims. As one graduate of Evergreen State wrote:

> [T]he integrated studies model at Evergreen is an extraordinary, powerful, and valuable medium. It was in the context of this model that I began to learn *new ways of thinking,* rather than simply collecting quanta of information as I had done (quite successfully) at the universities I previously attended. This is what I mean when I say that [this program] is the first place I got any *education* at all: Evergreen is the first place where I had the opportunity to integrate the bits and chunks of information I was collecting and to synthesize them into a new understanding of the world I live in, of myself, and of my role as a member of society. It is like the difference between collecting a pile of bricks and building a house. At the "regular" universities I attended I got a load of bricks which collected in piles that never added up to any coherent whole. At Evergreen, I was so intent upon building the house that the bricks just went into place without my having to memorize each one. . . .[36]

This is not an atypical evaluation. A participant in the FLC program at Stony Brook writes that "students soon learned that disciplinary perspectives are neither all encompassing truths nor arbitrary expressions of professors' personalities, but are orga-

nized methods of inquiry, each revealing and concealing different aspects of the issue under discussion. Thus students were
forced into making choices because the answers were not inherent in any one disciplinary method." This writer adds that the
program "also gave students the opportunity to articulate and
examine their own resistance to academic discourses. . . ."[37]

The authors of *Learning Communities* do not mention any programs in which recent conflicts over multiculturalism, the
humanities canon, and the politics of culture are taken as the
theme used to link courses. Such concerns should lend themselves readily to the learning community structure, however, and
they are taken up centrally in several programs recently under
way. At least one campus, Western College at Miami University
of Oxford, Ohio, made the political correctness debate the focus
of its freshman orientation week in 1991, with a packet of readings sent to participants several weeks in advance. According to
Miami science Professor William Newell, the event worked well
to acclimatize freshmen to intellectual discussion, in contrast
with the customary blandness of orientation week activities.[38]

Several programs have actually organized departmental or
college curricula around central controversies. One is a new major
in English and Textual Studies at Syracuse University. According to the department newsletter, the Syracuse program replaces
"a traditional pluralism" in which different viewpoints are separately represented, with a framework in which each position
"acknowledges its allied or contestatory relation to other positions."

The aim, as the newsletter puts it, is "not to impose one way
of knowing on everyone, but to make the differences between
ways of knowing visible" and to put in the foreground "what is
at stake in one way of knowing against another." The aim "is to
make students aware of how knowledge is produced and how
reading takes place and thus to make them capable of playing
an active role in their society, enabling them to intervene in the
dominant discourses of their culture." The Syracuse program

starts from the recognition that in standard curricula "faculty may disagree profoundly," but students find out about those disagreements only "by chance as they move from course to course. . . ." The implication is "that it is more important to master certain predesignated works organized by genres, periods, and authors than to inquire into the grounds of such categories or into the ends and means of reading." The new Syracuse curriculum tries to shift this emphasis without simply glorifying "a fashionable methodology or settling for a vapid pluralism as a way of defusing disagreements."[39]

No teacher at Syracuse is *forced* to enter the departmental dialogue. However, according to Steven Mailloux, the department chair who led the installation of the new program (he has since left the university), because the program is organized as a dialogue, any teacher's refusal to enter can be interpreted by students as itself a meaningful choice (not necessarily a discreditable one). Under the Syracuse plan, Mailloux writes, "a faculty member simply continuing to teach his course in a traditional, isolated way does not undermine the curricular 'conversation' because the curriculum causes his action to be read as a move in the conversation. Since students will be helped to 'read' their courses side-by-side, when they take a traditionalist course they will be able to read it through the grid of the new major."[40] It remains to be seen how well the conception will translate into practice, but the principle seems to me sound.

A similar "conflict model" informs the English program at Carnegie Mellon University, where both the English major and graduate programs are oriented toward "Literature and Cultural Studies" (with a strong option in rhetoric). According to former department head Gary Waller, students in standard programs are usually given "little or no acknowledgment that the contents and structures of the discipline [are] not given categories but culturally produced, always under debate, always sites of complex struggle." The goal at Carnegie Mellon is "to bring into debate a host of epistemologies, distinctive methodologies, issues,

188 Beyond the Culture Wars

problems, and challenges. . . ." Instead of "a polite pluralism," the aim is "an acknowledged clash of paradigms, frameworks, languages, and methodologies, with an understanding that . . . some will not survive the battle or that we will find ourselves led into conversations we didn't expect."[41]

The principle of making conflict the basis of community is also implicit in the World Studies Program at Queens College, New York, a freshman-sophomore general education program taught jointly by humanists and social scientists. According to one internal account of the program, instead of "treating works from and about different societies and cultures in isolation or simply as examples of variety, works shall be studied in relation to each other, each offering a commentary on the others. Consistently, in interpreting the material, emphasis shall be placed on understanding current debates between competing theories and disciplinary perspectives rather than studying only one position within those debates." The program addresses the debate, "for example, over the extent to which we live in a global economy . . . as opposed to national economic systems with important connections to one another; or the debate over representation itself, over how we represent or construct culture and society, how we 'read' and 'write' cultures."[42] It is too early to judge the success of the Syracuse, Carnegie Mellon, and Queens experiments. But their principles are at the least promising and ought to lend themselves to adaptation elsewhere without extra expense or increased bureaucracy.

I would like to round off this discussion of curricular integration strategies by outlining an idea that is not yet in widespread use but that seems to me to possess great potential, especially in cases where learning communities and thematic clustering do not prove feasible. This would be an adaptation of the academic conference or symposium to the needs of the undergraduate curriculum. One often senses in the heightened atmosphere of today's professional conferences that the eagerness with which these events are attended stems from the fact that they are providing the kind of intellectual community that is sadly missing from the home campus. Professors obviously believe that they learn a great deal from these conferences, which have become increasingly central in the education of graduate students (who have organized excellent conferences that I have attended at the universities of Wisconsin and St. Louis and at Ohio State University). Suitably adapted to the interests and needs of undergraduates, such conferences could be doing a lot to inject coherence and intellectual community into the undergraduate curriculum.

Today at almost every campus across the land there runs throughout the academic year a rich array of extracurricular conferences, lectures, and performances. These events often speak directly to the concerns of the courses being given at the time they occur, yet the events and courses are rarely synchronized. Indeed, these extracurricular events compete with the regular courses even though they are often on the same subjects. An opportunity is thus missed, since these events could be used to provide a common reference point for several courses. With a bit of advance planning, such events could be doing much to interrelate the pieces of the curriculum, without the need for exhausting faculty meetings or complicated administrative machinery. Departments and colleges could develop their own events to bring their courses together. Computer and videotechnology could help to overcome the logistical problems.

If several teachers in the same or different departments agreed to assign a common text in a particular semester, they could then organize a transcourse symposium in order to compare different approaches, clarify disputed issues, and give students a more dramatic sense of the wider debate on the issues than a single course can provide. Teachers on any campus are already randomly assigning many of the same texts without even knowing it (universities should be using their data banks to inform faculty of the texts being taught by their colleagues in a given year). Simultaneously assigning a text like *Nineteen Eighty-four*

in a literature, philosophy, and political science course would
create the opportunity for a joint discussion on those disputed
issues of truth, politics, and ideology that are polarizing so many
campuses: Is knowledge a creation of power or independent of
power? This discussion would then become a reference point
when the courses reconvened separately.

The current debate over multiculturalism would make an
excellent topic for such transcourse symposia. A symposium could
be organized for example around this thoughtful sample topic
from the Queens World Studies brochure: "Do women writing
poetry in Egypt, Latin America, and the United States have more
in common as women or as poets?"[43] The question neatly poses
the vexed issue of poetic and ethnic categories and thus invites
the kind of sorting out of claims and arguments that is badly
needed. One could imagine (budget permitting) one or two of
the poets being read in the course being invited to address the
symposium.

To combat the deadly syndrome in which teachers talk only
to other teachers and students remain passive spectators, students could be assigned varying roles in such a conference, ranging
from writing papers about it afterward (it becomes easier to write
about ideas when one is describing an actual event rather than
abstractions in a void) to giving some of the papers and responses
in it to eventually organizing and running the event themselves.I
have recently observed two remarkably successful student-run
conferences. One of these was a conference on Darwin and Gen-
esis—or the challenge of evolutionary science to traditional religion—in an NEH-supported freshman seminar program at the
University of North Carolina at Greensboro (entitled "Teaching
the Canon and the Conflicts"). The other was a conference on
the canon controversy organized by three graduate instructors
of freshman composition at the University of Illinois at Urbana.
What most impressed me besides the high quality of the student-run discussion and the high proportion of students who
took an active part in it was the way the students took respon-

sibility for the discussion instead of waiting for cues from their teachers.

In an extension of this idea, an entire academic semester could be given a theme. A semester could be organized around controversial issues such as "The Challenge to Traditional Culture." Such a tactic would give the semester an intellectual meaning and focal point around which communities could cohere. An academic semester conceived as a set of thematically focused events at which courses intersect has more definition and character than a set of more or less valuable courses that merely cover a spectrum of fields. It makes it possible for the semester to be actually *about* something, counteracting the aimlessness that conservatives justly attack, but without the need for a restrictively unified curriculum. Since the theme would change from semester to semester or year to year, an ossified canon would not be a danger and diverse interests could be satisfied. Common experience would be created without establishing a permanent canon.

To be sure, such transcourse conferences would entail meeting in larger groups than many of us feel comfortable with (the Greensboro freshman conference I attended combined four sections of the course or approximately a hundred students). In our legitimate reservations about large impersonal lecture courses, we are too prone to equate bigness with lifeless education. The question of bigness and smallness needs to be rethought in relation to the problem of intellectual community and the need for common experience. We often forget that the small-group instruction that we glorify comes at the expense of such common experience and that without common experience small-group discussion easily founders. At Greensboro it was not a question of replacing small with large groups but of using a large event to provide a common reference point when the students returned to their small sections. The students did not seem to feel alienated in the large event, knowing they would soon be discussing it in their smaller classes.

I am aware that to some the idea of drawing on the academic conference format in the way I propose would signal the final surrender of undergraduate education to precisely those forces that to them are most corrupting to academic life. Camille Paglia has even proposed the abolition of academic conferences and symposia, which for her epitomize the professionalism and opportunism that have drawn us away from true scholarship and teaching. What is interesting, however, is that Paglia offered this proposal at a conference, or at least a conferencelike public event, attended by more than seven hundred people.[44]

A recent series of campus debates on the culture war by Dinesh D'Souza and Stanley Fish have reportedly been attracting turnaway crowds sometimes numbering over a thousand. I have not attended any of these debates, and I am not sure they would fit my particular ideal of what such exchanges should be like. But from the reports I have received from students who have attended these events, nobody seems to have minded that they were large. On the contrary, I sense that the very size of the audience intensified the excitement at these events—as it is usually understood to do in most areas of life except education, where smallness is considered a prerequisite of goodness. It occurred to me that had one of the Fish-D'Souza debates been on my campus and I had assigned it to a class along with articles by the principals, the effect could only have been to enhance the work of the class. Even had the debate been disappointing, we would have acquired a useful reference point for our discussion.

The point is that large, even massive events are not necessarily incompatible with good education—not, that is, if they are *events* and not some lone professor mumbling over his lecture notes about Emily Dickinson's dates of birth and death. The aim in using such events would be not to do away with small classes and one-on-one teacher-student contact but to make them better by giving them some publicly shared experience to focus on. A campus at which hundreds or thousands had attended the same intellectual event would be a campus with something in common to talk about for a change beside the football or basketball team.

If educational considerations do not force us to think such thoughts, material ones may. If higher education is to pull out of the financial crisis it has been sliding into, administrators are going to have to rethink the relation of size to educational effectiveness—not, one hopes, in a spirit of capitulation to the cynical cutting of education funds by opportunistic politicians but in recognition that curricular disconnection is as wastefully expensive as it is pedagogically dubious. I noted in an earlier chapter that the glorification of the small intimate class as the ideal of sound education evolved during a period of affluence that enabled universities to expand the disciplinary playing field without thinking closely about the interrelations of the players. A shrinking economic base should force us to take these interrelations into account, as we should have long ago. It should be a question not of replacing smallness with bigness but of making intelligent use of bigness in order to get more benefit from smallness.

It should be possible to do more with the same commitment of resources. For turning courses into conversations in the ways I have described and suggested should not mean *adding* yet another task to the work of already overburdened teachers. The point is not to add more tasks to teaching but to take advantage of the missed chances for dialogue that are already latent in what teachers do every day. In the long run such an innovation would figure to make teaching less arduous by giving teachers a set of reference points outside their own classroom that they now, if they are conscientious, must laboriously reconstruct by themselves without help from their colleagues. In fact, it is hard to think of a better prescription for teacher burnout than a system of uncorrelated courses, which produces immense duplication of effort while depriving teachers of help from their colleagues. In such a system, teachers are at once overworked and underutilized.

I grant that an integrated curriculum will be only as good as the teachers who work in it; at its worst it will only inflict new kinds of boredom and alienation on students. A dull, pedantic faculty teaching in concert will produce no more inspiring result than a dull, pedantic faculty teaching separately. Instead of being turned off by a single instructor, students would be turned off by a whole phalanx of instructors. Even in this worst-case scenario, however, the outcome would probably be no worse than it can often be under the prevailing system. Then, too, for a generation now, hiring and promotion committees have gone to increased expense and trouble to recruit faculties that are not only intellectually gifted but more representative of the diversity of intellectual culture than in the past. So it does not seem unreasonable to assume that the average college faculty possesses a certain potential for intellectual liveliness. My assumption is that given such a faculty, it is more likely to realize its potential in a coordinated curriculum than in an uncoordinated one.

The reason for this assumption is that coordinated teaching has a built-in reality check that solo teaching lacks; this is because working together enables teachers to counteract and supplement one another's deficiencies. In a collective situation questions that challenge or redefine the premises of a particular classroom discussion would not arise in one class only to be dropped as the student goes to the next class. Such questions would have a chance to become part of other conversations besides the one that takes place in the privacy of a single course, thus sustaining and reinforcing the most pertinent questions.

In other words, the greater the degree of collective interaction, the greater the likelihood of generating and sustaining self-criticism of whatever in that interaction is problematic or debatable, including its relevance or the lack of it to students' needs. Given a faculty that is reasonably representative of the current diversity of academic culture, an integrated curriculum figures to be more theoretically, historically, and politically self-aware than a faculty that teaches in isolation. Instead of repressing the history and politics embedded in it, such a curriculum would tend to bring that history and politics into the foreground and open it to debate.

I HAVE suggested that what gives the integration experiments I have discussed here a hope of succeeding where their predecessors failed is that they do not set themselves against the dynamics of modern academic professionalism and American democracy but take these dynamics for granted as opportunities to be seized. They create a common ground of discussion without assuming the need for an overarching consensus on values.

Such a reorientation has become possible because the humanistic culture of the small college has increasingly become indistinguishable from the culture of the professional disciplines. Even small liberal arts colleges today are increasingly encouraging their faculties to contribute to the professional research community and to see their research as energizing their teaching rather than being in conflict with it. This development draws predictably bitter complaints from traditionalists like NEH Chair Cheney, who are unable to see the research spirit as anything other than the death of humanistic and educational values.[45] And fifty years ago they would have been right. Most academic research was so governed by narrow specialization and the cult of the positivistic fact that it had very little to contribute to general education or even to the undergraduate major. But as I argued in Chapter 6, this is no longer the case. The humanities would hardly be the cultural and political battleground they have become today if pedantic specialization were still the first order in its research. Whatever you may say about the turn the humanities have recently taken toward culture and politics, it is not devoid of relevance to life. I cannot speak for the sciences, but to judge from reports of declining student interest in that sphere, it seems likely that the sciences may also be forced to widen their scope to encompass more of their historical and social context.

In any case, a promising revaluation has been taking place of the potential of academic research for general education. What is significant about this development is that for the first time in the history of American mass education, it becomes possible to envision an end to the disastrous idea that making the curriculum more coherent and pertinent to the needs of students has to be a rearguard action against professionalism, research, and contemporary culture. By viewing their professional interests and debates as an enriching context for teaching rather than a paralyzing enemy of teaching, the programs I have discussed in this chapter suggest a way to overcome the perennial administrative stumbling block of integrated curricula, the difficulty of making courses cohere without either cumbersome red tape or a lockstep core curriculum that reduces diversity of choice in what to teach and study.

I began this chapter by quoting Leo Marx's recollection of how teaching our differences had been successful. Marx's conclusion merits the last word:

> [I]t seems unlikely that anything like a consensus on literature, culture, and the teaching of these subjects is likely to be attainable soon. Anyone who has experienced the theoretical perturbations of recent years would have had no illusions on that score. Perhaps the most interesting aspect of the current situation in the teaching of literature is in fact the extent of the differences that divide us.
>
> Unfortunately, we do not take sufficient advantage of those differences for pedagogical purposes. Instead of sharing them with students, using them for what they are, a source of interest, vitality, and direction, we usually keep them out of the classroom, as if they were one of the profession's truly embarrassing secrets. But why conceal our disagreements?[46]

Even as Marx wrote these words in the mid-1980s, a number of colleges were already starting to do what he recommended, and more are now joining in. If we are serious about reforming education, we will watch them.

Notes

Chapter 1: *Introduction: Conflict in America*

1. Roger Kimball, "Tenured Radicals: A Postscript," *New Criterion* 9, no. 5 (January 1991): 13.
2. Quoted in Benjamin De Mott, "The Myth of Classlessness," *New York Times* (October 10, 1990), p. A23.
3. I have traced these processes of conflict avoidance in the field of literary studies in my earlier book *Professing Literature: An Institutional History* (Chicago: University of Chicago Press, 1987), from which I draw at times in the present book.
4. I am indebted for this point to Susan Lowry of the University of Wisconsin at Milwaukee.
5. Recent articles have adduced evidence that at least one of the most sensational "PC stories" was baseless or grossly exaggerated. See Jon Weiner's account of the Stephan Thernstrom case at Harvard, "What Happened at Harvard," *Nation* 253, no. 10 (September 30,1991): 384–88; see also Rosa Ehrenreich, "What Campus Radicals?" *Harper's* 283, no. 1699 (December 1991): 57–61. These and other pieces challenging the reliability of widely circulated PC stories have recently been collected in Patricia Auferheide, ed., *Beyond PC: Toward a Politics of Understanding* (St. Paul, Minn.: Graywolf Press, 1992), pp. 92–121.

Chapter 2: *The Vanishing Classics*

1. Milton Rosenberg, "Uproar in the Academy: Deconstruction's Corrosive Role in American Higher Learning," *Chicago Tribune Books* (March 24, 1991), p. 5.

2. Dinesh D'Souza, *Illiberal Education: The Politics of Race and Sex on Campus* (New York: Free Press, 1991), p. 20.

3. Christopher Clausen, "It Is Not Elitist to Place Major Literature at the Center of the English Curriculum," *Chronicle of Higher Education* (January 13, 1988), p. A52.

4. William J. Bennett, "To Reclaim a Legacy," 1984 Report on Humanities in Education, *Chronicle of Higher Education* (November 28, 1984), pp. 1, 14–21.

5. Allan Bloom, *The Closing of the American Mind: How Higher Education Has Failed Democracy and Impoverished the Souls of Today's Students* (New York: Simon and Schuster, 1987).

6. Jonathan Yardley, "Paradise Tossed: The Fall of Literary Standards," *Washington Post,* "Style" (January 11, 1988), p. 52. The *Times* article to which Yardley refers was Joseph Berger, "U.S. Literature: Canon Under Siege," *New York Times* (January 6, 1988), p. B6.

7. David Brooks, "From Western Lit to Westerns as Lit," *Wall Street Journal* (February 2, 1988), p. 36.

8. William Bennett, quoted by Robin Wilson, "Bennett: Colleges' 'Trendy Lightweights' Replace Classics with Nonsense," *Chronicle of Higher Education* (February 10, 1988), p. A27.

9. Mark Helprin, "The Canon under Siege," *New Criterion* 7, no. 1 (September 1988): 36.

10. Terry Teachout, "Why Johnny Is Ignorant," *Commentary,* 85, no. 3 (March 1988): 71.

11. Lynne V. Cheney, *Humanities in America;* A Report to the President, the Congress, and the American People (Washington, D.C.: National Endowment for the Humanities, 1988), pp. 11–12.

12. D'Souza, *Illiberal Education,* p. 68. D'Souza slightly misquotes Clausen.

13. Cathy Davidson, " 'PH' stands for Political Hypocrisy," *Academe* 77, no. 5 (September–October 1991): 14.

14. John Searle, "The Storm over the University," *New York Review of Books,* XXXVII, no. 19 (December 6, 1990): 38–39. Two Stanford sources that support Searle's information and conclusions are Mary Louise Pratt, "Humanities for the Future: Reflections on the Western Culture Debate at Stanford," in *The Politics of Liberal Education,* ed. Darryl J. Gless and Barbara Herrnstein Smith (Durham, N.C.: Duke University Press, 1992), pp. 13–31; Bob Beyers, "Machiavelli Loses Ground at Stanford; Bible Holds Its Own," *Chronicle of Higher Education* (June 19, 1991), pp. B2, B3.

15. Searle, "The Storm over the University," p. 39.

16. Charles B. Harris, "The ADE Ad Hoc Committee on the English Curriculum: A Progress Report," *ADE Bulletin* 85 (Winter 1986): 26–27.

17. Bettina J. Huber and David Laurence, "Report on the 1984–85 Survey of the English Sample: General Education Requirements in English and the English Major," *ADE Bulletin* 93 (Fall 1989): 39.

18. Harris, "The ADE Ad Hoc Committee on the English Curriculum," p. 29.

19. Phyllis Franklin, Bettina J. Huber, and David Laurence, "Continuity and Change in the Study of Literature," *Change* 24 (January–February 1992): 42–48.

20. "MLA Survey Casts Light on Canon Debate," *MLA Newsletter,* 23 (Winter 1991): 12.

21. Arthur N. Applebee, *A Study of Book-Length Works Taught in High School English Courses* (Albany, N.Y.: Center for the Learning and Teaching of Literature, 1989), p. 16.

22. Chinua Achebe, "An Image of Africa: Racism in Conrad's Heart of Darkness," in Joseph Conrad, *Heart of Darkness,* 3d ed., ed. Robert Kimbrough (New York: W. W. Norton, 1988).

23. Joseph Conrad, *Heart of Darkness,* p. 37; quoted by Achebe, Ibid., p. 253.

24. Ibid., p. 253; Leavis's discussion appears in *The Great Tradition* (London: George W. Stewart, 1948; reprinted 1954), pp. 211–21.

25. Ibid., p. 256.

26. Ibid., p. 257.

27. Ibid.

28. Ibid., p. 261.

29. See, for example, the treatments of Conrad and *Heart of Darkness* in two influential works of Marxist criticism, Terry Eagleton's *Criticism and Ideology: A Study in Marxist Literary Theory* (London: New Left Books, 1977), pp. 130–40; and Fredric Jameson's *The Political Unconscious: Narrative as a Socially Symbolic Act* (Ithaca, N.Y.: Cornell University Press, 1983), pp. 206–80.

30. Frederick Crews, "The Strange Fate of William Faulkner," *New York Review of Books* XXXVIII, no. 5 (March 7, 1989): 49.

31. Dinesh D'Souza, "Illiberal Education," *Atlantic* 267, no. 3 (March, 1991): 52.

Chapter 3: *How to Save "Dover Beach"*

1. Matthew Arnold, "Dover Beach," in *The Poetical Works of Matthew Arnold,* ed. C. B. Tinker and H. F. Lowry (New York: Oxford University Press, 1950), p. 210.

2. George Will, "Literary Politics," *Newsweek* (April 22, 1991), p. 72.

3. Jerry Adler, "Taking Offense," *Newsweek* (December 24, 1990), p. 54.

4. James Atlas, *The Book Wars: What It Takes to Be Educated in America* (Knoxville: Whittle Direct Books, 1990), back dust jacket, adapted from p. 86. Published in revised form as *Battle of the Books: What It Takes to Be Educated in America* (New York: W. W. Norton, 1992).

5. Arthur M. Schlesinger, Jr., *The Disuniting of America: Reflections on a Multicultural Society* (New York: W. W. Norton, 1992). The quoted phrase comes from Schlesinger's article "When Ethnic Studies Are Un-American," *Wall Street Journal* (April 23, 1990): A14.

6. Bennett, "To Reclaim a Legacy," pp. 17–18.

7. Schlesinger, *The Disuniting of America,* pp. 137–38.

8. Joan A. Scott, "Liberal Historians: A Unitary Vision," *Chronicle of Higher Education* (September 11, 1991), p. B1.

9. Cynthia Ozick, "A Critic at Large: T. S. Eliot at 101," *The New Yorker* (November 20, 1989), pp. 119, 152. Part of the quotation comes from a letter by Ozick to the *New Criterion* 8, no. 8 (April 1990): 6.

10. W. J. T. Mitchell, "The Good, the Bad, and the Ugly: Three Theories of Value," *Raritan* 6, no. 2 (Fall, 1986): 63.

11. Anthony Hecht, "The Dover Bitch: A Criticism of Life," *The Hard Hours: Poems by Anthony Hecht* (New York: Atheneum, 1978), p. 17

12. Lynne V. Cheney, *Humanities in America,* p. 7.

13. Terry Eagleton, *Literary Theory: An Introduction* (Minneapolis: University of Minnesota Press, 1983), p. 7.

14. Robert Alter, *The Pleasures of Reading in an Ideological Age* (New York: Simon & Schuster, 1989).

15. Denis Donoghue, "The Joy of Texts," review of Alter, *The Pleasures of Reading, New Republic* 200, no. 26 (June 26, 1989): 17.

16. Henry Louis Gates, Jr., "On U.S. Cultural Literacy: The Stakes and Strategy," *New York Times* (December 6, 1989), p. 26. See also Gates's *Loose Canons: Notes on The Culture Wars* (New York: Oxford University Press, 1992), p. 118.

17. Diane Ravitch, "Multiculturalism: E Pluribus Plures," *American Scholar* 59, no. 3 (Summer 1990): 352.

18. Lawrence Lipking, "Canon Fodder," *New Republic* 205, no. 14 (September 30, 1991): 43.

19. Francis Oakley, "Against Nostalgia: Reflections on Our Present Discontents in Higher Education," in *The Politics of Liberal Education,* pp. 286–87.

    The 1991 report of the Association of American Colleges, entitled *The Challenge of Connected Learning,* states that "too often, faculty members view [their] debates as separate from their work as educators. Even as they address these issues in their scholarly journals and conferences, they withhold them from their students." The report urges "highlighting these strongly contested topics as well as the role of previously excluded groups in shaping these debates. . . ." (*The Challenge of Connected Learning* [Washington, D.C.: Association of American Colleges, 1991], p. 19.)

    Hugh B. Price, vice-president of the Rockefeller Foundation, asks whether it is "necessary to present all history as settled truth? Where there is sharp disagreement, . . . why not pose the contrasting positions to students as propositions to be studied? Teach them how to use primary sources, weigh evidence, critique arguments and form their own views." ("The Mosaic and the Melting Pot," *New York Times* [September 23, 1991], p. A17.)

Chapter 4: *Hidden Meaning, or, Disliking Books at an Early Age*

1. Mike Rose, *Lives on the Boundary* (New York: Free Press, 1989), pp. 46–47.

2. John Toren, letter, *New Republic* 201, no. 9 (August 28, 1989): 6, 41.

3. Bloom, *Closing of the American Mind,* p. 344.

4. Ibid., p. 375.

5. Richard Rorty, "That Old Time Philosophy," *New Republic* 198, no. 14 (April 4, 1988): 32.

6. Gordon Harvey, literature textbook forthcoming from Bedford Books of St. Martin's Press.

7. Patricia Bizzell writes, with respect to student writing generally: "Students often complain that they have nothing to say, whereas 'real-world' writers almost never do, precisely because real-world writers are writing for discourse communities in which they know their work can matter, whereas students can see little purpose for their own attempts . . . other than to get a grade." "Cognition, Convention and Certainty: What We Need to Know About Writing," *PRE/TEXT* 3 (Fall 1982): 232. See also Kenneth A. Bruffee, "Collaborative Learning and 'The Conversation of Mankind,' " *College English* 46, no. 7 (November 1984): 635–52: John Trimbur, "Collaborative Learning and Teaching Writing," in B. W. McClelland and T. R. Donovan, eds., *Perspectives on Research and Scholarship in Composition* (New York: Modern Language Association, 1985), pp. 87–109.

8. Gregory Jay, unpublished manuscript.

9. Rose, *Lives on the Boundary*, p. 181.

10. Alter, *Pleasures of Reading in an Ideological Age*, pp. 16–17.

11. Cleanth Brooks, "The New Criticism," *Sewanee Review* 87, no. 4 (Fall 1979): 593.

Chapter 5: *"Life of the Mind Stuff"*

1. Willie Morris, *North toward Home* (Boston: Houghton Mifflin, 1967), pp. 149–50.

2. Charles Hall Grandgent, "The Dark Ages," *PMLA* 28, no. 4, appendix (1912): p. l.

3. Helen Lefkowitz Horowitz, *Campus Life: Undergraduate Cultures from the End of the Eighteenth Century to the Present* (Chicago: University of Chicago Press, 1987), pp. 56–81; Robert Maynard Hutchins, *The Higher Learning in America* (New Haven: Yale University Press, 1936), p. 2.

4. Michael Moffatt, *Coming of Age in New Jersey: College and American Culture* (New Brunswick, N.J.: Rutgers University Press, 1989), n. 29, p. 321.

5. Ibid., p. 272.

6. Rose, *Lives on the Boundary*, p. 187.

7. Ibid., p. 188.

8. Ibid.

9. Rewley Belle Inglis et al., eds., *Adventures in American Literature*, 4th ed. (New York: Harcourt, Brace, 1948), p. iii.

10. Lynne V. Cheney, "The Stanford Reading List Debate," *Washington Post* (February 16, 1988), p. A19.

11. Editorial, "Dangerous Mischief in Academe," *Chicago Tribune* (January 7, 1991), sec. 1, p. 12.

12. Ron Grossman, "Hitting the Books," *Chicago Tribune* (January 2, 1991), sec. 3, pp. 1–2.

13. Andrew Ross, *No Respect: Intellectuals and Popular Culture* (New York: Routledge, 1989), p. 157.

14. George Orwell, "Raffles and Miss Blandish," in *The Collected Essays, Journalism and Letters of George Orwell*, vol. 3, ed. Sonia Orwell and Ian Angus (New York: Harcourt

Brace & Javonovich, 1968), pp. 212–24; "Boys' Weeklies," *Collected Essays,* vol. 1, pp. 460–85; and "The Art of Donald McGill," *Collected Essays,* vol. 2, pp 155–65.

15. This point has been made by David Shumway in "Reading Rock 'n' Roll in the Classroom," in *Schooling and the Politics of Culture,* ed. Henry Giroux and Peter MacLaren (Albany: State University of New York, 1992), p. 232.

16. F. R. Leavis, *Education and the University* (London: Chatto & Windus, 1972; first published 1943), p. 138; cited in William Cain, "Argument," *English* 35 (Summer 1986): 184.

17. Edward Curran quoted by Karen Lawrence, "Curriculosclerosis: Or, Hardening of the Categories," *ADE Bulletin,* 90 (Fall 1988): 16.

18. Gregory Jay, unpublished essay. Some of Jay's ideas have appeared in "The First Round of the Culture Wars," *Chronicle of Higher Education* (February 26, 1992), pp. B1–2.

Chapter 6: *Other Voices, Other Rooms*

1. Gayle Green, "The Myth of Neutrality, Again?" in *Shakespeare Left and Right,* ed. Ivo Kamps (New York: Routledge, 1991), p. 24.

2. Diana Fuss, *Essentially Speaking: Feminism, Nature and Difference* (New York: Routledge, 1989), p. 105.

3. Thomas S. Kuhn, *The Structure of Scientific Revolutions,* 2d ed. (Chicago: University of Chicago Press, 1970), p. 150.

4. Gregory Colomb, *Disciplinary "Secrets" and the Apprentice Writer: The Lessons for Critical Thinking* (Upper Montclair, N.J.: Montclair State College, Institute for Critical Thinking, 1988), pp. 2–3.

5. For this point I am indebted to an unpublished talk by Susan Lowry.

6. I am indebted for this point to Susan H. McLeod, "Writing across the Curriculum: An Introduction," forthcoming in *Writing across the Curriculum: A Guide to Developing Programs,* eds. McLeod and Margot Soven (Newberry Park, Calif.: Sage, 1992).

7. I adapt an observation made in a somewhat different context by Mary Louise Pratt, "Humanities for the Future: Reflections on the Western Culture Debate at Stanford," in *Politics of Liberal Education,* p. 19.

8. Joseph Tussman, *Experiment at Berkeley* (New York: Oxford University Press, 1969), p. 6.

9. Ibid., p. 11.

10. I fail to do justice here and elsewhere in this book to a popular and valuable innovation that goes under the name of "collaborative learning" and is identified with work by Ken Bruffee, John Trimbur, Andrea Lunsford, Lisa Ede, and others. I agree with much of this work but believe that its logic points to something beyond "the classroom" as the locus of dialogue. On collaborative learning, see the essays by Bruffee and Trimbur mentioned in n. 7 to Chapter 4; see also Andrea Lunsford and Lisa Ede, *Singular Texts/Plural Authors: Perspectives on Collaborative Writing* (Carbondale, Ill.: Southern Illinois University Press, 1990).

11. Bloom, *Closing of the American Mind,* p. 338.

12. Ibid., p. 339.

13. I have developed this argument about "the myth of specialization" at greater length in two articles: "The Scholar in Society," forthcoming in *Introduction to Scholarship in Modern Languages and Literatures*, ed. Joseph Gibaldi (New York: Modern Language Association of America, 1992), pp. 343–62; and "Academic Writing and the Uses of Bad Publicity," *South Atlantic Quarterly* 91, no. 1 (Winter 1992): 5–17.

14. Rose, *Lives on the Boundary*, p. 197.

15. An encouraging sign of a move in this direction is the so-called undergraduate research movement, which has been supported by the Association of American Colleges in Washington, D. C.

Chapter 7: *Burying the Battlefield, or, a Short History of How the Curriculum Became a Cafeteria Counter*

1. David Richter, private correspondence.

2. Bennett, "To Reclaim a Legacy," pp. 19–20.

3. Ravitch, "Multiculturalism," pp. 337–38.

4. Frank Gaylord Hubbard, "The Chairman's Address," *PMLA* 28, no. 4, appendix (1913): lxxxi. Here and in the rest of this chapter I reframe arguments and materials from my *Professing Literature: An Institutional History* (Chicago: University of Chicago Press, 1987).

5. Oliver Farrar Emerson, "The American Scholar and the Modern Languages," *PMLA* 24, no. 4, appendix (1909): xcviii–cxix.

6. Ibid.

7. Bliss Perry, *And Gladly Teach* (Boston: Houghton Mifflin, 1935), p. 243.

8. Laurence R. Veysey, *The Emergence of the American University* (Chicago: University of Chicago Press, 1965), p. 311.

9. Ibid., p. 258.

10. Ibid., p. 308.

11. Ibid., pp. 337–38.

12. Gary F. Waller, "Powerful Silence: 'Theory' in the English Major," *ADE Bulletin* 85 (Winter 1986): 33.

13. For more on the coverage model, see my "Taking Cover in Coverage," *Profession 86* (New York: Modern Language Association of America, 1986): 41–45; and "What Should We Be Teaching—When There's No 'We'?," *Yale Journal of Criticism* 1, no. 2 (Spring 1988): 189–211.

14. Robert Scholes, *Textual Power: Literary Theory and the Teaching of English* (New Haven: Yale University Press, 1985), p. 58.

Chapter 8: *When Is Something "Political"?*

1. Orwell, "Why I Write," *Collected Essays,* vol. 1, p. 4.
2. F. O. Matthiessen, *American Renaissance: Art and Expression in the Age of Emerson and Whitman* (New York: Oxford University Press, 1968; first published 1941), p. ix.
3. Alfred Kazin, *On Native Grounds: An Interpretation of American Prose Literature* (New York: Reynal and Hitchcock, 1942; reprinted 1982), pp. 400–01.
4. John Searle, " 'The Storm over the University': A Further Exchange," *New York Review of Books* XXXVIII, no. 9 (May 16, 1991): 63. Searle's comments were made in two exchanges with me in the letters column of the *Review.*
5. Jonathan Dollimore and Alan Sinfield, eds., *Political Shakespeare: New Essays in Cultural Materialism* (Ithaca, N.Y.: Cornell University Press, 1985), p. vii.
6. Searle, "The Storm over the University," p. 35.
7. Searle, "A Further Exchange," p. 63.
8. Ibid.
9. Letters to the Editor, *Chronicle of Higher Education* (March 11, 1992), pp. B4–5; the original article appeared as "What Has Literary Theory Wrought?" *Chronicle of Higher Education* (February 12, 1992), p. A48.
10. Joseph Epstein, "A Case of Academic Freedom," *Commentary* 82, no. 3 (September, 1986): 39.
11. When Granville Hicks was let go by Rensselaer, an investigation by the American Association of University Professors concluded that "it is difficult to avoid the inference that Professor Hicks would have been dealt with otherwise, but for his economic and social beliefs." But the dismissal was not reversed, and Hicks left teaching. This, however, was before the more serious witch-hunts of the 1950s. For documentation of this and numerous other accounts, see Ellen W. Schrecker's *No Ivory Tower: McCarthyism and the Universities* (New York: Oxford University Press, 1986), pp. 65–66 and passim.
12. Brander Matthews, *An Introduction to the Study of American Literature,* rev. ed. (New York: American Book Company, 1896), pp. 10–11.
13. John Churton Collins, *The Study of English Literature: A Plea for Its Recognition and Reorganization at the Universities* (New York: Macmillan, 1891), pp. 11–12.
14. Sir Henry Newbolt, quoted by Chris Baldick, *The Social Mission of English Criticism, 1848–1932* (New York: Oxford University Press, 1983), p. 104.
15. On the early resistance to American literature, see Kermit Vanderbilt, *American Literature and the Academy: The Root, Growth, and Maturity of a Profession* (Philadelphia: University of Pennsylvania Press, 1986).
16. James W. Tuttleton, "Rewriting the History of American Literature," *New Criterion* 5, no. 3 (November 1986): 3.
17. Fred Lewis Pattee, quoted by Pattee, in *Penn State Yankee* (State College, Pa.: Pennsylvania State University Press, 1953), p. 314.
18. Albert Kerr Heckel, quoted by Carol S. Gruber, *Mars and Minerva: World War I and the Uses of the Higher Learning in America* (Baton Rouge: Louisiana State University Press, 1975), p. 239.

19. Herbert E. Hawkes, quoted ibid., p. 244.

20. Edward R. Turner, quoted ibid., p. 241.

21. William A. Frayer, ibid.

22. Charles Mills Gayley, *Shakespeare and the Founders of Liberty in America,* cited in Benjamin P. Kurtz, *Charles Mills Gayley* (Berkeley: University of California Press, 1943), p. 129.

23. Jacket copy, Herman Melville, *Moby-Dick: or, The Whale* (New York: Collier Books, 1962).

24. Jacket copy, James Fenimore Cooper, *The Prairie: A Tale,* Signet Classic (New York: New American Library, 1964).

25. Henry Louis Gates, Jr., "The Master's Pieces: On Canon Formation and the African-American Tradition," *Politics of Liberal Education,* p. 103.

26. Michael Kinsley, "P.C. B.S.," *New Republic* 204, no. 20 (May 20, 1991): 8.

27. William A. Henry III, "Upside Down in the Groves of Academe," *Time* (April 1, 1991), p. 66.

28. Michael Bérubé, unpublished manuscript.

29. Eve Kosofsky Sedgwick, "Jane Austen and the Masturbating Girl," *Critical Inquiry* 17, no. 4 (Summer 1991): 818.

30. Dinesh D'Souza, *Illiberal Education,* p. 162.

31. Joseph Epstein, "The Academic Zoo: Theory—In Practice," *Hudson Review* 44, no. 1 (Spring 1991): 17.

32. Michael Bérubé, "Political Correctness and The Media's Big Lie," *Village Voice,* xxxvii, no. 25 (June 18, 1991): 32.

33. George Will, "Literary Politics," p. 72.

34. Kinsley, "P.C. B.S.," p. 8.

35. Fredric Jameson, *The Political Unconscious, p. 291.*

36. *Editorial, New Republic,* special issue "Race on Campus," 204, no. 20 (February 18, 1991): 8.

37. For an illuminating discussion of recent debates on "essentialism," see Diana Fuss, *Essentially Speaking.*

38. Toni Morrison, "Unspeakable Things Unspoken: The Afro-American Presence in American Literature," *Michigan Quarterly Review* 28, no. 1 (Winter 1989): 19.

39. Stephen Greenblatt, "Opinion," *Chronicle of Higher Education* (June 12, 1991), p. B3.

40. William Shakespeare, *The Tempest,* ed. Frank Kermode (New York: Methuen, 1954), I, ii, 333–34.

41. Ibid., iii, 40–42.

42. Ibid., iii, 51–52.

43. D. H. Lawrence, *Studies in Classic American Literature* (New York: Viking Press, 1961; first published 1923), pp. 4–5; Greenblatt discusses Caliban in *Learning to Curse: Essays in Early Modern Culture* (New York: Routledge, Chapman and Hall, 1990), p. 24ff.

44. See for example Martinique playwright Aimé Césaire's *A Tempest* (New York: Ubu Repertory Theater Productions, 1986).

45. Orwell, "Politics and the English Language," in *Collected Essays,* vol. 4, pp. 127–140.

46. Gregory Jay, unpublished manuscript.
47. Chinua Achebe, quoted by Bonnie Auslander, "The Writer as Statesman and Troublemaker," *Daily Hampshire Gazette* (February 24, 1988), pp. 19–20.
48. Will, "Literary Politics," p. 72.
49. Lynne V. Cheney, quoted by Christopher Myers, "Government and Politics," *Chronicle of Higher Education* (April 10, 1991), p. A22.
50. Lynne V. Cheney, quoted in "Personal and Professional," *Chronicle of Higher Education* (January 30, 1991), p. A15.
51. Richard Cohen, "Iannone: A Political Choice," *Washington Post* (July 9, 1991), p. A19.
52. Theodore Roth, "Law and Economics," *University of Chicago Magazine* 83, no. 6 (August 1991): 28.
53. Robert Kuttner, "The Tyranny of the Economically Correct," *Washington Post* (April 8, 1991), p. A17.
54. On right-wing funding of the culture war, see Jon Wiener, "The Olin Money Tree: Dollars for Neocon Scholars," *Nation* 250, no. 1 (January 1, 1990): 12–14; Donald Lazere, "Political Correctness Left and Right," *College English* 54, no. 3 (March, 1992): 79–88.
55. John Taylor, "Are You Politically Correct?," *New York* (January 21, 1991), pp. 32–40.
56. Wiener, "What Happened at Harvard," 384–88.
57. Harvey C. Mansfield, Jr., quoted by Karen J. Winkler, "Portrait," *Chronicle of Higher Education* (October 16, 1991) p. A5.
58. Terry Eagleton, *Ideology: An Introduction* (London: Verso, 1991), p. xiv.

Chapter 9: *Turning Conflict into Community*

1. Leo Marx, "Teaching Our Differences," unpublished paper.
2. Ron L. Hamberg, letter, *Chronicle of Higher Education* (March 13, 1991), p. B5.
3. Quoted in *Federated Learning Communities: The Best of Both Worlds*, a program guide to SUNY—Stony Brook, p. 6.
4. John Dewey, *Democracy and Education: An Introduction to the Philosophy of Education* (New York: Free Press, 1944; first published 1916), p. 249.
5. Tussman, *Experiment at Berkeley*, p. 57. Also worth mentioning is the ""Correlated Curriculum" sponsored in the late thirties by the National Council of Teachers of English. See NCTE volume *A Correlated Curriculum: A Report of the Committee of the National Council of Teachers of English*, ed. Ruth Mary Weeks (New York: Appleton-Century, 1936).
6. Tussman, pp. 33.
7. Ibid., pp. 3ff.
8. Ibid., p. xiv.
9. Ibid.
10. Ibid.
11. Programs based on the earlier model still continue at small colleges such as St. John's College, Annapolis, and are from time to time praised as emplars by critics like

former Secretary Bennett. For reasons suggested in this chapter, they seem to me incapable of serving as a general solution.

12. William H. Newell, ed., *Interdisciplinary Undergraduate Programs: A Directory* (Oxford, Ohio: Association for Integrative Studies, 1986); Faith Gabelnick, Jean MacGregor, Roberta S. Matthews, and Barbara Leigh Smith, *Learning Communities: Creating Connections among Students, Faculty, and Disciplines* (San Francisco: Jossey-Bass, 1990).

13. For a survey of interdisciplinary theory and practice, see Julie Thompson Klein, *Interdisciplinarity: History, Theory, and Practice* (Detroit: Wayne State University Press, 1990).

14. Lawrence Hussman, "The Faculty's Forte: 'Team Teaching' the Literature Survey," *ADE Bulletin* 99 (Fall 1991): 29, 32.

15. Ibid., p. 32

16. Ibid.

17. Ibid.

18. Ibid., p. 30.

19. See Graff, "What Should We Be Teaching—When There's No 'We'?"

20. Gabelnick et al., *Learning Communities,* p. 19.

21. Ibid., p. 43.

22. Ibid., p. 24.

23. Seattle and Bellevue Community College courses, described in report of the Washington Center for the Improvement of the Quality of Higher Education, *Final Report to the Ford Foundation,* 1986–88 vol. 1 (Olympia, Wash.: Evergreen State College, 1988), p. 20.

24. Susan L. Feagin and Burton L. Dunbar, "Interdisciplinary Studies in the Humanities: An Experiment in Interdisciplinary Teaching," *Humanities Education Connections* (Fall 1989): 26.

25. Ibid., p. 21.

26. Ibid., p. 22.

27. Gabelnick et al., *Learning Communities,* p. 64.

28. Patrick J. Hill, "Medium and Message in General Education," *Liberal Education* 67, no. 2 (1981): 142.

29. Ibid., p. 136.

30. Hill, "Communities of Learners: Curriculum as the Infrastructure of Academic Communities," *In Opposition to Core Curriculum: Alternative Models of Undergraduate Education,* ed. J. W. Hall and B. L. Kelves, (Westport, Conn.: Greenwood Press, 1982), p. 121.

31. Ibid., p. 119.

32. Hill, "Medium and Message," p. 140.

33. Hill, "Communities," p. 122.

34. Ibid., p. 131.

35. Gabelnick et al., *Learning Communities,* p. 64.

36. Student comment, quoted by Office of Institutional Research, *1988 Alumni Survey Results* (Olympia, Wash.: Evergreen State College, 1989), p. 27.

37. Stephen Olsen, private correspondence.

38. William Newell, private correspondence.

39. Syracuse University, *English Newsletter* 1, no. 1 (March 1990): 3.
40. Steven Mailloux, private correspondence.
41. Gary Waller, "Polylogue: Reading, Writing, and the Structure of Doctoral Study in English," unpublished departmental material.
42. Unpublished internal documents: World Studies Program, Queens College, New York.
43. *World Studies,* Queens College program brochure.
44. Camille Paglia, quoted by Thomas C. Palmer, Jr., "Bearding the Literary Lions in Their Den," *Boston Globe* (March 20, 1992), p. 19.
45. Lynne V. Cheney, *Tyrannical Machines: A Report on Educational Practices Gone Wrong and Our Best Hopes for Setting Them Right* (Washington, D.C.: National Endowment for the Humanities, 1990).
46. Marx, "Teaching Our Differences."

Index

Cheney, Lynne V., 20, 52, 98, 103, 121, 165, 167, 195
Chicago, University of, 66, 89, 111, 183
Chicago Tribune, 16, 17, 98
Chronicle of Higher Education, 17, 148, 167, 172
City College of New York, 34
class, social, 4, 22
classical languages, 95, 96, 128–29, 152
classics (great books), 16–36, 48–49, 66, 72, 95, 96, 128–29, 130, 151, 152, 153–54, 175
Clausen, Christopher, 17–21
Clifford, James, 160
Cliffs Notes, 66, 76
Closing of the American Mind, The (Bloom), 72, 93, 118
cognitive dissonance, 12–14, 106–24, 117
Cohen, Richard, 165
Collins, John Churton, 204*n*.13
Colomb, Gregory, 111
colonialism, *The Tempest* and, 160–163
Color Purple, The (Walker), 16–25, 34, 36, 97
Columbia University, 132, 154
Coming of Age in New Jersey (Moffat), 90
Commentary, 19, 149, 168
"common culture," 41–47, 62, 126, 136, 165
community, integrated curriculum and, 171–96
conferences, academic, 188–93
    multiculturalism and, 190
Conrad, Joseph, 15, 51, 96
conservatives, 5, 30, 48, 128
    affirmative action criticized by, 88
    "common culture" as viewed by, 41–47
    curriculum as viewed by, 10–11
    neo-, 60, 101, 153
    politics and, 35, 126, 142, 144, 147, 157, 165–170
    see also humanists; traditionalists
Cooper, James Fenimore, 155
course descriptions, 22–24
course system, as bureaucracy, 114–18, 122
Course fetish, 114–24
Crawford, Joan, 99
creative writing, 137
Crews, Frederick, 31–32
critical debates, *see* debates
Critical Inquiry, 81
critical vocabulary, *see* jargon
cultural literacy, 88, 110, 113
cultural studies, 13, 142, 169
Curran, Edward, 103
curriculum:
    classical Greek and Latin, 95, 96, 128–29, 152
    classics in, 16–36, 48–49, 66, 72, 95, 96, 128–29, 130, 151, 152, 153–54, 175
    consensus on, 58, 120, 125, 134–135, 178
    as conversation, 57, 108–9
    cultural nationalism and, 150–52
    difficulty of, 97–104
    disjunction of, 13–14, 57–62, 105–124

history of, 125–43
history of politics in, 149–56
integrated, 171–96
live-and-let-live philosophy of, 10
multiculturalism and, 4, 22, 34, 42, 45–47, 60, 159–60, 167, 186, 190
politics and, 25–26, 142–43, 168
post-Civil War controversy on, 152
"Cynthia Ozick's Farewell to T. S. Eliot— and High Culture" (Kramer), 49*n*

Dances with Wolves (movie), 6
Dante Alighieri, 72, 73, 74
Dartmouth Review, 166
Davidson, Cathy, 21
Davis, Bette, 99
Dead Poets Society, The (movie), 116
debates:
    as conversation, 70–71, 74
    critical, 66–69, 70–71, 74, 77
    on curriculum, 11–15, 37–41, 54, 58–59, 60, 109, 126, 139–40, 171
    on literary canon, 52, 54–59, 60, 94–97, 190
    on literary theory, 54, 56–63
    students' awareness of, 106–14
deconstructionism, 34, 35, 69, 72, 137, 158
de Kruif, Paul, 65
de Man, Paul, 158
department, defined, 116
Derrida, Jacques, 158
Dewey, John, 174–75
Dickens, Charles, 24, 99
Dickinson, Emily, 117
Dictionary of Cultural Literacy (Hirsch), 88, 110
Dietrich, Marlene, 99
Directory of Interdisciplinary Programs, 179
"discourse community," 75
Disuniting of America, The: Reflections on a Multicultural Society (Schlesinger, 42
Doctorow, E. L., 168
Dollimore, Johnathan, 204*n*.5
Donoghue, Denis, 56
Do the Right Thing (movie), 6
"Dover Beach" (Arnold), 37–40, 44, 47, 49, 51, 52
"Dover Bitch, The" (Hecht), 51
Dreiser, Theodore, 96
Dryden, John, 108
D'Souza, Dinesh, 17, 20–21, 22, 34, 157, 166, 192
Duke University, 21, 157, 167
Dunbar, Burton L., 182

Eagleton, Terry, 53, 54, 159, 169
Ede, Lisa, 202*n*.10
Ehrenreich, Rosa, 197*n*.5
elective system, 129
Eliot, Charles William, 129
Eliot, George, 24
Eliot, T. S., 48, 67, 108, 144
Ellison, Ralph, 85, 94